Sacred India

SACRED INDIA

This edition 2002, first published 1999
Published by
Lonely Planet Publications Pty Ltd ABN 36 005 607 983
90 Maribyrnong St, Footscray, Victoria 3011, Australia
World Wide Web: www.lonelyplanet.com or AOL keyword: *lp*

Lonely Planet Offices
Australia: Locked Bag 1, Footscray, Victoria 3011
USA: 150 Linden Street, Oakland, CA 94607
UK: 10A Spring Place, London NW5 3BH
France: 1 rue du Dahomey, 75011 Paris

Many of the photographs in this book are available for licencing from Lonely Planet Images.
email: lpi@lonelyplanet.com.au
Web site: www.lonelyplanetimages.com

ISBN 1 74059 366 9
A catalogue record for this book is available from the National Library of Australia

Foreword © William Dalrymple 1999
Photographs © individual photographers 1999
Text, maps and line illustrations © Lonely Planet Publications Pty Ltd 1999

Printed by The Bookmaker International Ltd
Printed in China

SACRED INDIA

Foreword by William Dalrymple

lonely planet

CONTENTS

FOREWORD

It was a high, clear, Himalayan morning and we were corkscrewing our way up from the banks of the river Bhagirathi, along the steep sides of a thickly wooded valley. The track was soft and mossy and it led through ferns and brackens, thickets of brambles and groves of tall Himalayan cedar trees. Small waterfalls tumbled through the deodars. It was May and after a ten-day trek, I was just one day's walk from my destination: the great Himalayan temple of Kedarnath, believed by Hindus to be one of the principal homes of Lord Shiva and so in some ways a Hindu Mount Olympus.

I was not alone on the road. The previous night I had seen groups of pilgrims — mainly villagers from Rajasthan — camping beside the temples and bazaars at the bottom of the mountain, warming their hands over small driftwood fires. Now, in the light of morning, their numbers seemed to have miraculously multiplied. Indeed the narrow mountain track now appeared like a great sea of Indian humanity: every social class from every corner of the country was there. There were groups of farmers, illiterate holy men and urban sophisticates from North and South all rubbing shoulders like something out of a modern Indian Canterbury Tales. The rich rode horses or were carried up in doolies, a strange cross between a wicker deck chair and a rucksack, but the vast majority of poor pilgrims had no option but to walk.

Every half mile we would come across groups of twenty or thirty villagers straining up the steep mountain path. Barefoot, bent-backed old men with grey walrus moustaches would be leading their heavily veiled wives up the slopes; others, more pious, would be bowed in

prayer before the small shrines — often no more than piles of pebbles and a calendar poster of Shiva — which were strung out at intervals along the route. I fell in with one group of farmers from a village near Jaipur. Why had they come on this pilgrimage, I asked. Was it for a holiday?

'No,' replied Ram Bihari, who turned out to be the village headman. 'We have come to do darshan — to catch a glimpse of God — in the miraculous image of Shiva in the temple at Kedarnath. Every year people from our district come here to pray and each time their prayers are answered.'

'What are you personally praying for?' I asked.

'A son,' replied Ram Bihari. 'My wife has given birth to four daughters and still I have no heir.'

'And did you never think of coming before?' I asked.

'For many years I have wanted to make this journey,' he replied. 'But it is expensive to travel: this pilgrimage will cost nearly three thousand rupees. But at last God has allowed me to make it here. Many members of my family have joined together to help me financially, especially my brother. He is looking after my fields while I am away. In return I will pray for him when I get to the temple.'

Sadhus, India's wandering holy men, also filled the road in dazzling profusion. As I wandered through the knee-high columbines, buttercups and wild strawberries of the high-altitude pastures, I passed a constant stream of lean, dark, wiry men with matted, dreadlocked hair and thick beards leaping up the track. Some travelled in groups of two or three; others travelled alone and many of these appeared to be locked in deep meditation as they walked. They were as fit and as hardy as mountain goats, even though some were weighed down by heavy metal tridents, the outward sign of their inward dedication to Lord Shiva. For the Himalaya here are understood to be Shiva's domain, and like him, the sadhus who trek up here consciously turn their back on society and its rules, in an effort to find moksha (salvation) in the clear air and crystal silence of the mountains.

A full thirty kilometres separated Kedarnath from the previous night's camp at the bottom of the mountain. After six hours climbing we crossed the treeline, passing over a saddle of rock onto a desolate plain of scree and snow. Some of the villagers were barefoot, while others were wrapped only in plastic sheeting. Most had never seen snow before and few had ever experienced a night at this altitude or had any idea what to expect when they arrived.

Eventually, we turned the side of the saddle and there, ahead of us, surrounded by the white flanks of the Kedarnath peaks, stood the temple. In the eyes of Hindus, the shrine is one of the supreme residences in India of Lord Shiva. For if Uttarakhand, the region through which we were passing, means in Sanskrit 'The Land of the Gods', it is also, more particularly, the Land of Shiva. Indeed the very stones of the Himalaya are understood to be Shiva's matted locks and his presence is inescapable in the geography as he sits meditating on the peak at Kedarnath.

For this reason Hindus see the temple at Kedarnath as a tirtha, a crossing place between different worlds, linking the profane to the sacred. The pious pilgrim who steps into the temple here enters a ford between different states of perception, where you can cross from the world of men to the world of the gods as easily as you might cross a slow-flowing stream at the height of the dry season. Here your prayers are more quickly heard, and your desires more readily fulfilled. In Hindu thought, there are many thousands of tirthas all over India, any of which

is capable of giving access to the divine. Some such as Kedarnath are famous across the country; others are known only to the villages that surround them. But between them, this vast network of keyholes into the divine constitutes the very essence of India's sacredness, indeed it is arguably the very essence of India's 'Indianness'. As the great Sanskritist, Diana Eck, puts it: 'Considering its long history India has had but a few hours of political and administrative unity. Its unity as a nation, however, has been firmly constituted by the sacred geography it has held in common and revered: its mountains, forests, rivers, hilltop shrines.'

For to Hindus, as also to many Indian Buddhists, Muslims, Christians and Sikhs, India is a Holy Land. The actual soil of India is thought by many simple rural Hindus to be the residence of the divinity and, in villages across India, is worshipped and understood to be literally the body of the Goddess, while the features of the Indian landscape — the mountains and forests, the caves and outcrops of rock, the mighty rivers — are all understood to be her physical features. She is Bharat Mata, Mother India, and in her main temple in Varanasi the Goddess is worshipped not in the form of an idol but manifested in a brightly coloured map of India. Her landscape is not dead but alive, dense with sacred significance.

There is a Hindu myth that seeks to explain this innate holiness. According to the legend, Rajah Daksha, the father-in-law of Shiva, failed to invite his son-in-law to an important sacrifice. Overcome by shame, the rajah's daughter, Sati, jumped into a fire and killed herself. Shiva, inconsolable, traversed India in a furious, grief-stricken dance, carrying her body. The gods became anxious that Shiva's anguish would destroy the universe, so they dispersed her body bit by bit, across the plains and mountains and forests of India. Wherever fragments of her body landed, there was established a tirtha, often a shrine to the Goddess, and in time many of these tirthas became major pilgrimage sites.

The legend encapsulates a picture of India as a mythologically charged landscape whose holy pilgrimage sites are as widely distributed as the body of Sati itself. The idea of India's sacredness is therefore not some Western concept grafted onto the subcontinent in a fit of mystical Orientalism: it is an idea central to India's conception of itself. Indeed this idea of India as a sacred landscape predates classical Hinduism, and, most importantly, is an idea that was in turn passed onto most of the other religions that came to flourish in the Indian soil.

The origins of the idea of Sacred India seem to lie in India's ancient pre-Vedic religions where veneration was given to sprites known as nagas or yakshas. These godlings were associated with natural features of the landscape such as pools and sacred springs and the roots of banyan trees, and were believed to have jurisdiction over their own areas. Over the centuries, the myths associated with such features changed, so that a particular sacred pool might in time come to be associated with Ram and Sita, or a mountain linked with Krishna or the wanderings of the Pandava brothers of the Mahabharata. Just as the sacredness of the landscape percolated from pre-Vedic and tribal folk cults into classical 'Great Tradition' Hinduism, so in the course of time the idea slowly trickled from Hinduism into Buddhism, Sikhism, Indian Christianity and even Indian Islam.

Nowhere else in Islam are there so many Sufi shrines where individual pilgrims can come and directly gain access to the divine through the intercession of the saint of a particular village or mohalla. Mosques are everywhere in Islam, but Sufi shrines are, in a very specific way — and very like Hindu tirthas — fords linking one world with the next. They are, moreover, places where, thanks to the intervention of a great saint, you can cross over from the realm of the human to the realm of the divine, a place where prayers are somehow simply more likely to be answered.

Like Hindu tirthas, Sufi shrines are linked by a formal pilgrimage circuit and at different times of the year you can see hundreds of thousands of pilgrims massing for the anniversary of the saint's death. The greatest of all is the 'Urs of

the great thirteenth-century Delhi saint, Shaikh Hazrat Nizam-ud-din Aulia Chisti. Nizam-ud-din promised his followers that if they loosened their ties with the world, they could purge their souls of worries and move towards direct experience of God. After all, said the saint, all existence and all religions are one. Prayer and fasting were for the pious — but the Divine Presence was everywhere. What was important, he maintained, was not the external ritual of the mosque or Hindu temple, but simply to understand that divinity can best be reached through the gateway of the human heart. We all have paradise within us, said the saint, if we know where to look.

In this way the Sufis succeeded for the first time in bringing together Muslim and Hindu in a movement that spanned the gulf separating the two very different religions: one ordered and austere, the other profoundly fluid and colourful. For Sufism, with its holy men and visions, its emphasis on the individual's search for union with God and, above all, in its idea of sacred space, has always borne remarkable similarities to the popular practice of Hinduism. To this day the shrine of Nizam-ud-din still attracts almost as many Hindu, Sikh and Christian pilgrims as it does Muslims.

Even Indian Christianity has taken on this very Indian idea of the sanctity of the landscape. Anyone who travels in Kerala at Easter time is likely to see busloads of Christian pilgrims heading for Malayattur, a holy mountain associated with Apostle Thomas, the 'Doubting Thomas' of the Gospels, who in Malabar is universally believed to have brought Christianity to India. Every year, tens of thousands of St Thomas Christians climb Malayattur wearing saffron lungis and singing hymns to St Thomas while carrying wooden crosses on their backs. Like Hindu pilgrims on their way to Kedarnath, the pilgrims see Malayattur as a kind of trap door in the heavens, a place where no prayer can be ignored, and to which they can bring their most profound yearnings and desires. Outwardly, what happens at Malayattur is a Christian pilgrimage, but the particular form the pilgrimage takes, the intensity of the veneration of the sanctity of a holy mountain, and the ritual vocabulary of the pilgrims' actions are all an inheritance from ancient Indian tradition that makes the pilgrimage quite unlike any other expression of Christianity you are ever likely to see.

It is in pilgrimage, in travelling from holy site to holy site, from tirtha to tirtha, that the sacredness of India is best celebrated and experienced. For a Western traveller, it is also as good a way as any to ease yourself into the real soul of India. I for one will certainly never forget travelling down from Kedarnath and falling into conversation with a sadhu of about my own age. I had always assumed that most of the holy men I had seen in India were from traditional village backgrounds and were motivated by a blind and simple faith. But as soon as we began talking it became apparent that Ajay Kumar Jha was in fact highly educated.

Ajay and I walked together along the steep ridge of a mountain, with the great birds of prey circling the thermals below us. I asked him to tell me his story and after some initial hesitation, he consented:

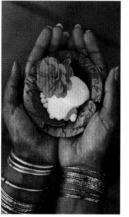

'I have been a sanyasi [wanderer] only for four and a half years,' he said. 'Before that I was the sales manager with Kelvinator, a Bombay consumer electricals company. I had done my MBA at Patna University and was considered a high flyer by my employers. But one day I just decided I could not spend the rest of my life marketing fans and fridges. So I just left. I wrote a letter to my boss and to my parents, gave away my belongings to the poor, and took a train to Varanasi. There I threw away my old suit, bought these robes and found a monastery.'

'Have you never regretted what you did?' I asked.

'It was a very sudden decision,' replied Ajay. 'But I have never regretted it for a minute, even when I have not eaten for several days and am at my most hungry.'

'But how did you adjust to such a change in your life?' I asked.

'Of course at first it was very difficult,' he said. 'But then everything worthwhile in life takes time. I was used to all the comforts: my father was a politician and a very rich man — by the standards of our country, at least. But I never wanted to live a worldly life like him. Now for the first time I have found peace.'

We had now arrived at the top of the ridge and the land fell steeply on every side. Ajay gestured out over the forests and pastures laid out at our feet, a hundred shades of green framed by the blinding white of the distant snow peaks:

'When you walk in the hills your mind becomes clear,' he said. 'All your worries disappear. Look! I carry only a blanket, a water bottle, and a few necessities. I have no possessions, so I have no worries.'

He smiled: 'Once you learn to restrain your desires,' he said, 'anything becomes possible.'

As we walked on, the track descended and the landscape became bleaker and more rocky. Below us, the Bhagirathi changed colour: from ash-grey at the bottom of the mountain it grew darker until, a little before our destination, it turned as black as essence of damsons. At lunchtime, as I brought out a sandwich, Ajay produced some food — rice and a few vegetarian dishes in a stack of tin tiffin bowls which we shared.

He said: 'To walk every day is a good life. But to walk in the Himalaya thinking of God: that is the best life. Men feel good when they live like this.'

WILLIAM DALRYMPLE
15TH APRIL, 1999

Hinduism

Hinduism is possibly the only 'religion' named after a place – the Indus River. Traces of Hinduism go back three thousand years and it is the largest religion in Asia today. Some 80 per cent of India's population, about 740 million people, are Hindus.

Hinduism defies attempts to define it. Some would argue that it is more an association of religions. It has no founder, central authority or hierarchy. It is not a proselytising religion. You can't be converted; to be a Hindu you must be born one. The very orthodox maintain that only a person born in India of Hindu parents can truly claim to be Hindu.

To outsiders Hinduism often appears a complex mix of contradictory beliefs and multiple gods. Although beliefs and practices vary widely from region to region, there are several unifying factors. These include samsara (common beliefs in reincarnation), karma (conduct or action), dharma (appropriate behaviour for one's station in life) and the caste system.

Caste is the basic social structure of Hindu society. Hindus are born into one of four varnas, or castes: Brahmin (priests), Kshatriya (warriors), Vaisya (merchants) and Sudra (peasants). These are subdivided into myriad hierarchical jati, or groups of 'families'. Beneath the four main castes are the Dalits, formerly known as Untouchables. Caste oversees and polices dharma – the doing of one's duty according to one's own caste, and in relation to other castes. Communal welfare, not individual rights, is the goal.

Pipal tree with garlands and puja offerings. The sacred pipal is thought to represent Brahma.

Essentially, Hindus believe in Brahman. Brahman is eternal, uncreated and infinite; everything that exists emanates from Brahman and will ultimately return to it. The multitude of gods and goddesses are merely manifestations — knowable aspects of this formless phenomenon. The deity worshipped by any one individual is often a matter of personal choice or of tradition at a local or caste level. The Hindu pantheon is said, according to the scriptures, to comprise 330 million devas, or gods. Theoretically, no beliefs or forms of worship are rejected by Hinduism, as all are aspects of Brahman. Brahman has three main representations or trimurti: Brahma, Vishnu and Shiva.

Brahma only plays an active role during the creation of the universe. The rest of the time he is in meditation and is therefore regarded as an aloof figure, unlike Shiva and Vishnu. His consort is Saraswati, goddess of learning, and his vehicle is a swan. He is sometimes shown sitting on a lotus that rises from Vishnu's navel, symbolising the interdependence of the gods. He is generally depicted with four (crowned and bearded) heads, each turned towards one of the four points of the compass. One of Brahma's days equates to 8640 million human years. Following one hundred Brahma years, the universe, and Brahma himself, dissolves, only to manifest again.

The lotus, according to Hindu beliefs, emerged from the primeval waters connected to the mythical centre of the earth through its stem. Often found in the most polluted of waters, it blossoms above them. The centre of the lotus corresponds to the centre of the universe, the navel of the earth; all is held together by the stem and the eternal waters. This is how Hindus are reminded their own lives should be – like the fragile yet strong lotus, a passage of beauty and strength.

Shiva, the destroyer, is the agent of death and destruction without which growth and rebirth could not take place. He is represented with either one or five faces, and four arms which may hold fire, a drum, a horn or a trident, or take the positions of protection or action. He is often surrounded by an arch of flame, for example, as Nataraja, Shiva of the Cosmic Dance, and sometimes he has a third eye. His matted hair is said to carry Ganga, the goddess of the river Ganges, in it.

Shiva's consort is Parvati, the beautiful. Parvati is the daughter of the Himalaya and is considered the perfect wife. She is also a form of the mother goddess Devi, whose body is India and who also appears as Durga, the terrible, and Kali, the fiercest of the gods.

New deities continue to emerge, for example Santoshi Mata, a figure created in a Bollywood film. Claimed to descend from Shiva and Parvati, she has been absorbed into the pantheon as a bona fide goddess. Women appeal to her for success in the modern urban world: help with improving a husband's flagging career, for example, or the acquisition of a refrigerator or radio.

An elderly Bengali lady, when asked what religion meant to her, said, simply but emphatically: Shiva. 'Other gods and goddesses are important but Shiva is the most important. Shiva is the root of everything: construction, destruction and preservation. Shiva is happy in a second and angry in a second. He is easily pleased. You don't have to spend a lot of money to please Shiva,' she added with a smile.

Susan Mitra

Arvind Singh Mewar described himself as a 'trustee of the state of Udaipur on behalf of Eklingji'. Eklingji is a form of Shiva. Every Monday (the auspicious day of Shiva), Arvind Singh Mewar pays homage to his personal family deity. The Maharana is the seventy-sixth custodian of the 1400-year-old House of Udaipur which, according to Hindu mythology, traces its origin to the sun. 'We have always regarded ourselves as transitory regents, not divine rulers, as representatives of the people in front of God.'

Sarina Singh

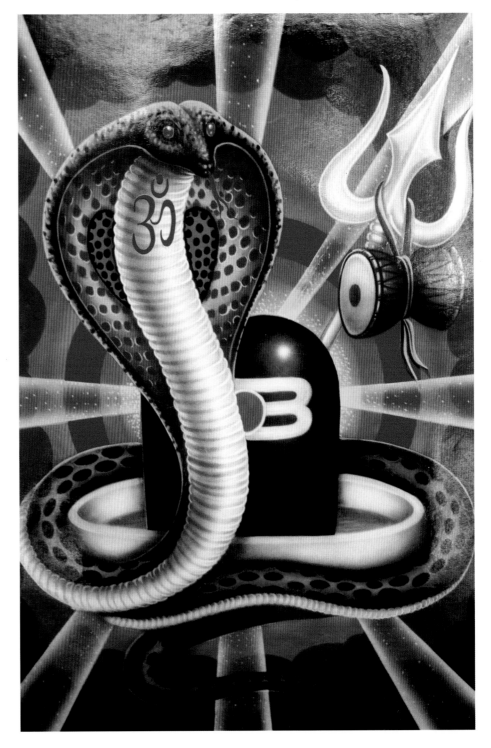

Shiva's throat is often depicted as blue, a result of drinking the poison that rose during the churning of the oceans at the beginning of creation.

LEFT
Shiva's creative role is phallically symbolised by his representation as the frequently worshipped lingam.

Kali – the black, the fiercest form of Shiva's wife, packaged ready to go

Durga is the goddess even the gods worship. She is Shakti, the power and strength of Brahma, Vishnu and Shiva. The gods, it is said, were impotent to quell a powerful demon in the guise of a black water buffalo. When their combined wrath condensed, it became female — the goddess Durga. To her each of the gods gave his most powerful weapon. She decapitated the buffalo-demon and slew the devil within.

Durga created Kali, the hideous goddess who sprang fully formed from Durga's forehead. Kali has four arms that hold a bloody sword, dangle a head by its scalp, confer blessings and exhort the followers not to be afraid. To incur the wrath of Kali is a fearsome mistake.

A Kali devotee. Kali is worshipped on the blackest nights of the lunar cycle. Her most famous temple is in Kolkata (Calcutta) – the Kalighat, from which the city takes its name. Every morning goats are sacrificed at the temple to satisfy the goddess' bloodlust.

Vishnu, the preserver or sustainer, is associated with 'right action'. He behaves as a lawful, devout Hindu, and protects and sustains all that is good in the world. In some ways Vishnu is similar to Christ — he is considered the redeemer of humanity. He sits on a couch made from the coils of the serpent-king Ananta and in his hands he holds a conch shell and a discus. Vishnu's vehicle is the half-man, half-eagle Garuda. Vishnu's consort is the beautiful Lakshmi, who came from the sea and is the goddess of wealth, prosperity, honour and love. She is often represented sitting on a lotus flower.

Vishnu has had nine incarnations, including Rama, Krishna and Gautama Buddha, and it is said that he will come again.

The Ramayana is the story of Rama's battle with the demon-king Ravana. Rama's consort is Sita, and his brother Lakshmana and servant Hanuman, the monkey god, are also widely worshipped.

Krishna's story is told in the epic Sanskrit poem, the Mahabharata, the longest work of literature in the world, which includes the Bhagavad Gita, a dialogue about the nature of duty. Krishna's mischievous nature, his peasant background and his legendary exploits with the gopis (milkmaids) have made him one of the most popular gods. His consorts are Radha (the head of the gopis), Rukmani and Satyabhama. Krishna is often blue and plays a flute.

It was through Krishna that the concept of bhakti, devotion to a personal god, was incorporated into Hindu philosophy. Immobilised on the eve of the great battle of Mahabharata at the thought of having to slay his own kinsfolk, Arjuna, one of the Pandava brothers, turned to his charioteer — who happened to be Krishna — for advice. Krishna asserted that it was Arjuna's dharma, or duty, as a Kshatriya (member of the warrior caste), to fight. He then added that one should pursue one's dharma not through introspection and reflection, but with detachment from the outcome. Only then could God act through the individual. This detachment could only be attained by surrendering the self (the ego) in devotion to a personal diety, an aspect of the supreme deity.

For sale: Krishna and other images

Ganesh is the elephant-headed god of prosperity and wisdom, and is probably the most popular of all the gods. He is the son of Shiva and Parvati, and his vehicle is a rat.

According to one legend, Ganesh, the god of good beginnings, had an inauspicious start. Born to Parvati in Shiva's absence, Ganesh grew up without knowing his father. One day as he stood guard while his mother bathed, Shiva returned and asked to be let into Parvati's presence. Ganesh stood his ground and refused to budge. Enraged, Shiva cut off Ganesh's head, only to discover that he had killed his own son. He resolved to replace Ganesh's head with the head of the first live creature that he came across. This happened to be an elephant — and Ganesh received the elephant's head. Parvati lamented that no one would worship Ganesh as he had lost all his godlike features. Shiva then decreed that no prayers would begin without first invoking Ganesh and so it has been since.

Kumutali, a district of Kolkata (Calcutta), is devoted to producing clay statues of Hindu gods for families and businesses to celebrate religious festivals and occasions.

These statues are moulded in clay, left to dry for a few hours and then painted and dressed in colourful material; the more expensive ones are clothed in embroidered silk. They take roughly between three and seven days to make, depending on the size and detail. The bigger, more elaborate ones are mainly bought by large organisations such as colleges and entertainment clubs. Most Hindu families together with singers and musicians buy statues of Saraswati for puja (worship) during Vasant Panchami Festival (Spring Festival). The statues are taken home for puja, after which they are immersed in the sacred Ganges River together with offerings, where they disintegrate.

Clay statues of Hindu gods including Ganesh and Saraswati in different stages of preparation, Kolkata

For many Hindus no day is complete without a visit to a mandir ('doorway to the heart', a Hindu temple), and no life complete without a pilgrimage to a sacred shrine. There are no fixed days or times to visit the temple. Some temples dedicated to particular gods are visited more on a certain day of the week. Hanuman devotees throng together on Tuesdays, Shiva gets most offerings on Mondays and Durga has an entire fortnight dedicated to her. Mandir doors open before sunrise and close after sunset. The priest conducts a formal prayer at opening and closing time on behalf of the community and assists in individual rituals throughout the day.

Sometimes people will go to the mandir simply for puja, but more often to cajole, plead with and even bribe the deities enshrined there for everything from excellent exam grades, a baby boy or a new car to peace and prosperity for the whole world. Prayers can be spoken, chanted and sung, or remain unspoken. Devotees believe that the presiding deity will always listen if all rituals have been followed diligently and with humility.

Images of the beautiful Shore Temple at Mamallapuram, Tamil Nadu

For Hindus, the square is the perfect shape (a circle is not considered perfect because it implies motion), so temples are always based on a square ground-plan. Extremely complex rules govern the siting, design and building of each temple, based on numerology, astronomy, astrology and religious law. These rules are so complicated and so important that it is customary for temples to house their own calculations as though they were religious texts.

The Dravidian temples of South India are notable for their striking architecture. The central shrine is topped by a vimana, a pyramidal tower several storeys high. One or more entrance porches lead to the shrine, around which is a series of courts, enclosures and pools known as tanks. The whole complex is surrounded by a high wall with entrances through enormous, magnificently sculpted gateways called gopurams, most of which are completely covered with sculptures of gods, demons, mortals and animals.

ABOVE
An elaborately sculpted gopuram teems with life, as crowded and busy as any Indian city street.

RIGHT
Devotees ring brass bells upon entering the temple to attract the deities' attention.

Meenakshi Shrine
This is the inner sanctum where the image of the goddess is enshrined, visible only in the puja firelight. In the north-east corner is the bed chamber, where the deities are united each evening.

Gopurams
These enormous, nine-storey-high gateway towers are decorated with thousands of celestial and animal figures.

Kilikattu Mandapam
Dravidian temples are renowned for their columned halls, known as 'thousand pillared halls'. The Kilikattu Mandapam has numerous intricately carved pillars.

Vambuthurar Gopuram
This gopuram, with over 450 sculptures, marks the entrance to the Meenakshi shrine.

Golden Lotus Tank
Devout pilgrims bathe in this tank whilst visiting the temple. On the western side of the tank is the mirror chamber where, each Friday evening, images of Shiva and Meenakshi are placed on a swing and gently rocked.

MEENAKSHI TEMPLE
MADURAI

The Meenakshi Temple in the southern Indian city of Madurai is a spectacular pastiche of Dravidian architecture. The enormously popular and powerful fish-eyed goddess Meenakshi (an incarnation of Shiva's wife) is the deity and protector of Madurai. The gopurams (enormous gateways) that tower over her temple are visible from almost every point in the city. The shrine housing the deity dates from the twelfth century.

Kalyan Mandapam
The marriage of Shiva and Meenakshi is celebrated in this mandapam in a spectacular festival each April/May.

Ashta Shakti Mandapam
Most people enter the temple at the southeast corner through this mandapam, or pillared pavilion, and proceed directly to the Meenakshi shrine to honour the goddess. Originally this hall was a choultry, where pilgrims ate and rested.

Meenakshi Naiker Mandapam
A small connecting mandapam leads to the forty metre high Meenakshi Naiker Mandapam, which was once the stables of the temple's camels and elephants.

Hampi, the famous site of the ruined city of Vijayanagar, is a special place for Hindus. Its religious significance draws Hindu pilgrims like this man from all over India to pray in its temples and marvel at the magnificence of Vijayanagar art. Its serene ambience — amid a haunting boulder-strewn landscape dotted with remnants of the rise and fall of one of the largest Hindu empires — draws travellers and holds them in its spell.

LEFT
The whitewashed Hanuman Temple, perched on a prominent hill overlooking Hampi's Sacred Centre, is visible for miles around.

The festival of Makhasankranti is celebrated throughout India. On this day, the sun god Surya is worshipped. It is considered very auspicious to bathe in rivers or tanks on this day and to give alms to the poor.

Sanjay Gupta comes to Dakshineswar Temple on the day of Makhasankranti each year. He was shivering. 'I went for a bath (in the Ganges) just now. It was nothing special for me as we often bathe in the Ganges. I was in the river for some time, about half an hour.' He offered me some prasaad (food that has been blessed by God) from a small banana-leaf dish he was holding. I wondered what he was thinking about while he was in the river. 'I was thinking of the gods and …beautiful movie actresses,' he said with a sidewards grin. Becoming serious, he said: 'I believe in God and every once in a while I should come to the temple and be reminded of God.'

SUSAN MITRA

ABOVE
This man visits the temple regularly to distribute food to the poor. He organises a formal queue of people to make sure that everyone receives a fair share.

LEFT
Outside many Hindu temples, stalls sell all kinds of religious paraphernalia, such as statues like these.

RIGHT
Women dry their saris after bathing in the Ganges.

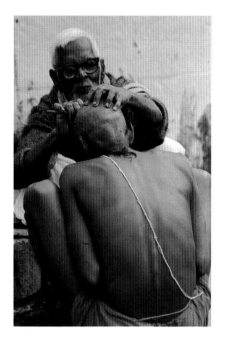

Brahmins, who belong to the priestly caste, inhabit the priviliged position at the top of the caste hierarchy.

'I have to replace my sacred thread every two to three months. It's made of cotton and becomes worn out as it's never removed even when I bathe. I am a Brahmin and I have to worship the thread by repeating mantras three times a day for at least ten minutes. My father showed me what to do. I feel that the worship improves my mind.'

INDRA NATH BANERJEE

A Brahmin priest mused on his feelings about being a priest: 'Brahmins are the facilitators for any important occasion. I didn't want to work as a priest. I did a Bachelor of Science degree, but I can't get work in my chosen field. So now I'm doing priestly work. I mostly perform domestic pujas. The family asks me to perform the ceremony to clear the way of obstacles. I don't set a fee, the family decides how much they will pay. If a well-off family pays poorly I will not perform any more ceremonies for them. Often the poorer families give more than the better-off families. I'm going to study astrology sometime in the future. I'll get more work if I know astrology because an astrologer is required whenever a child is born.'

SUSAN MITRA

LEFT

This Brahmin priest has been performing pujas for Hindu families in Kolkata for the last forty-five years. After puja, the priest accompanies the family to the Ganges River where the offerings are placed in the sacred waters. The puja tray holds chandan (sandalwood) paste, chawal (rice), supari (betelnut), tulsi (basil) leaves, honey and ganga jal (water from the holy Ganges River).

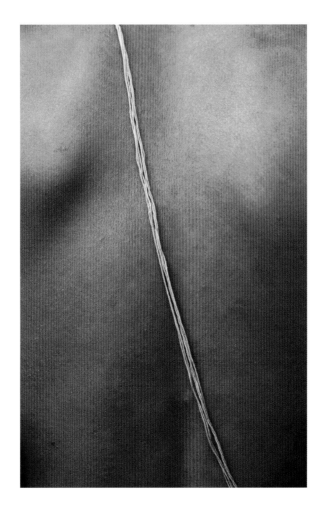

The Himalaya is revered as Dhev-bumi, the home of the gods. Devout Hindus derive great spiritual merit by undertaking pilgrimages to mountains such as Nanda Devi, and to holy shrines such as the Amarnath Cave.

At the full moon in the month of Sravana (July/August) tens of thousands of Hindu pilgrims make the arduous yatra (pilgrimage) to the Shri Amarnath Cave high in the western Himalaya. At this time, a naturally occurring ice formation reaches its greatest size. It is considered a lingam, symbol of Shiva.

'I've been to many religious places. I'm interested to see how people perform religious ceremonies. I like to be part of a congregation and meet various types of people with different ways of thinking. However, I didn't want to go to Amarnath purely for religious reasons. I very much wanted to see the scenery as well.

We went to Amarnath in August 1987. The ninth of August was an auspicious day, it was the full moon, and that was the day we saw the deities. My husband was not keen to make this journey because he thought it was too treacherous. A person cannot make the Amarnath pilgrimage unless God pulls you there. Everyone is welcome at Amarnath: Muslims, Christians and Hindus. The pony owners are Muslims and they are very good people.

It's extremely cold and we had to sleep in our clothes with lots of blankets. Sadhus and many other people bathe in the icy cold water on the approach to the cave, but we didn't.

I had dreamt of visiting Amarnath for a very long time. I stood at the viewing spot at the entrance to the cave for two minutes. It was worth the journey.'

MITALI MITRA

ABOVE
Pilgrim on the road to Amarnath. Around her neck can be seen a string of 108 beads; these garlands are known as rudraksh malas, and are characteristic of devotees of Shiva.

LEFT
The beautiful Nanda Devi mountain is believed to be a form of the goddess Nanda Devi who is the presiding deity of Uttarakhand in the Indian Himalaya. She is revered by the people who live within the shadow of the mountain.

'My wife wanted to visit Amarnath very much. I didn't want to go. It's a treacherous journey. It takes three days to go up the mountain and two days to come down. You can only visit Amarnath in the summer months because it's snowbound and the roads are impassable at other times. It's a very hazardous journey. Many people have died making this pilgrimage.

Eventually I gave in to my wife's wishes. We camped two nights in tents. We travelled by pony along a narrow, windy switchback road. I had two accidents: the first was when my pony slipped and I fell off; the second was when my pony almost fell off the side of the gorge. My wife says that was my punishment because I didn't want to go in the beginning.

The chief priest who leads the procession of pilgrims comes from Kashmir. He carries the Chardi Mubarak trishul (silver trident). After him follow the naga babas (naked sadhus). It takes more than an hour to walk the last two kilometres. There were times when I thought of abandoning the journey and going back. The pilgrims on their way down from the cave gave us encouragement to continue.

Once we had arrived at the entrance to the cave, the crush to see the deity was tremendous. I had to protect my wife. I was so flabbergasted that I forgot to see the deities. My wife told me to go back to the viewing area, so again I had to face the crush. The deities were made of ice. Shiva was in the middle, Parvati on one side and their son Ganesh on the other.

It was amazing, it was like I could see the whole of India from this small place on the mountain top.'

HITEN K. MITRA

I made my first pilgrimage about eighty years back. My parents took me to Kashi (Varanasi). We bathed in the Ganges, and along with many other pilgrims offered silver and gold coins to Lord Shiva.

I went back to Kashi maybe thirty-five, forty years ago, again to see Lord Shiva. Do you know that according to our Hindu mythology, Lord Shiva brought the Ganges from Mount Kailash to India? I crossed the Ganges by boat. I poured ganga jal over Lord Shiva's head and offered him food, sweets and silver coins. I also carried water from the Ganges back with me to Calcutta (Kolkata).

Nihar Bala Mitra

Kalighat Temple, in the old part of Kolkata (Calcutta), is an important pilgrimage site. According to legend, this is where the finger of Shiva's wife, Sati, landed. Sati self-immolated in protest against an insult to Shiva by her father. Shiva, grief-stricken, picked up the charred remains and began a cosmic dance that threatened to destroy the universe. To prevent this, Vishnu dismembered Sati's body and the pieces were scattered across India.

There were busloads of pilgrims stopping at Kalighat Temple on their way to a mela (fair). They had an ecstatic look in their eyes. They were shouting the names of God as the line surged forward and rocked back.

There were two lines of pilgrims to see the deity. The slow lane was for those who wanted a proper look at the deity, and the express lane was for those who were satisfied with a fleeting glimpse. Most were in the slow lane. We were taken to the side entrance by the temple priest. Two men, our bodyguards, pushed their way into the crowd, held hands and started to create a space for us to progress our way, slowly, to the front of the viewing platform. There was lots of shouting and jostling; it was like being in a small boat on rough seas.

We finally made our way to the front where there was a rope barrier. If the rope hadn't been there we would have fallen off the four-foot-high platform. Suddenly one of our guards jumped down. I could see him ducking, weaving and using his elbows to reach the deity, pushing all other hands and bodies away so that we could see the sacred flame. He looked up at us; we nodded and smiled back. He quickly returned, pleased and proud with his work.

The priest later explained to us that each person has a minute at the rope in which to see the deity and then they have to move on.

SUSAN MITRA

RIGHT
As the fiercest of the gods, it makes sense to propitiate the goddess Kali accordingly. Here at her most famous temple, the Kalighat in Kolkata, pilgrims bearing baskets of offerings queue to have darshan (an audience) with the deity.

Arches of peacock feathers dance on pilgrim shoulders. Frenzied women engage in a cajoling interplay with the rhythms and sounds of the musicians. And thousands of pilgrims surge forward in a state of ecstasy planting lighted camphor on the temple steps.

This is Thaipusam, the time for penance. After one month's fast from most foods and sexual pleasures, devotees come to implore Murugan (the second son of Shiva and Parvati) to absolve their bad karma. They ask for forgiveness for the sins of their past lives, or entreat the deity to cure their sick children. They vow to suffer pain, in return for desired outcomes.

They carry the feathers of the lord's vehicle — the peacock — and carry sweet milk to offer and appease him. As they reach his shrine their chants crescendo: 'Kartikiya, Kartikiya' (another of Murugan's names). They believe that this god of war, this warrior of youth and virility, is all powerful to accede to their requests.

Teresa Cannon

Pushkar lures the greatest flow of pilgrims on the auspicious full-moon day of Kartik Purnima (October or November), when thousands of devotees congregate around the lake and wash away their sins by taking a holy dip. Apart from pilgrims, during this time the town is also flooded with camels, cattle, tribal people and tourists, who come to take part in the world's most spectacular camel fair.

'Quite frankly, I didn't expect to see anything other than a lot of camels and hippies in Pushkar,' said 47-year-old Jeanette from New York. 'I really had no idea that this fair had any religious connections and for me it's the sadhus with their Bob Marley hairstyles and painted bodies that have been the icing on the cake.'

Just several weeks after returning home from a whirlwind trip in India, 24-year-old Ben made a snap decision to go back to India — but this time, indefinitely. 'For the first time in my life I am tuning in to my inner voice and that's why I have thrown in my graphic design career in London — this is the beginning of my spiritual search and I will stay here for as long as it takes to find myself.' Basing himself in Pushkar, Ben is just one of thousands who are drawn here with the sole intent of pursuing spiritual solace. 'Looking back, my life in the UK was so routine, so mechanical...so meaningless. My family thought I was crazy to abandon my cosy life in London, but I have found a peace in Pushkar that I have never experienced before and I'm not giving that up.'

SARINA SINGH

Devout Hindus visit the important pilgrimage centre of Pushkar at least once in their lives. According to legend, the sacred lake of Pushkar sprang up at the spot where Brahma dropped a lotus flower from the sky. Brahma wanted to perform a holy sacrifice at the lake on a full-moon night. Since his wife, Savitri, did not attend, he impetuously married another woman named Gayatri. The betrayed Savitri bitterly vowed that Brahma would not be worshipped anywhere other than Pushkar. Indeed, Pushkar is one of the only sites dedicated to Brahma in the world.

RIGHT
Camel trader at the Pushkar camel fair

LEFT
Camel camp at the Pushkar camel fair

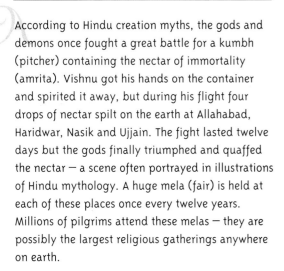

Sadhus throng a bridge over the Ganges at the Kumbh Mela, Haridwar, 1998. At an auspicious moment determined according to precise astrological calculations, pilgrims, in their thousands, converge on the river to bathe in its sacred waters. Crossing the bridge are the naga babas, the naked sadhus, their bodies smeared with ash from cremation fires to constantly remind them of their mortality. They have precedence over the other pilgrims and are first to enter the water.

According to Hindu creation myths, the gods and demons once fought a great battle for a kumbh (pitcher) containing the nectar of immortality (amrita). Vishnu got his hands on the container and spirited it away, but during his flight four drops of nectar spilt on the earth at Allahabad, Haridwar, Nasik and Ujjain. The fight lasted twelve days but the gods finally triumphed and quaffed the nectar — a scene often portrayed in illustrations of Hindu mythology. A huge mela (fair) is held at each of these places once every twelve years. Millions of pilgrims attend these melas — they are possibly the largest religious gatherings anywhere on earth.

The tika is a forehead marking with which most Hindu women adorn themselves. On a man it is referred to as a tilak, although these days the word tika has become common for both sexes. The mark takes many forms, and can be applied as a sign of blessing.

Tika is usually made from red vermilion paste (sindoor), white sandal-wood paste or ash (vibhuti), and can be used to denote sects. They can be roughly divided into two main groups: three horizontal bars indicate the person is a Shaivite (follower of Shiva); vertical stripes indicate a Vaishnavite (follower of Vishnu). The central stroke on a Vaishnavite's forehead is usually red, representing the radiance of the goddess Lakshmi (the wife of Vishnu in his incarnation as Narayan).

The small dot which women and girls place on their foreheads is known as a bindi. These are usually bought ready-made from the market and have become a fashion accessory, with every imaginable shape and colour to match the occasion.

One of Hinduism's most venerated signs is 'om'. Pronounced 'aum', it is an important mantra (sacred word or syllable). The '3' shape symbolises the creation, maintenance and destruction of the universe. The inverted crescent (half-moon or chandra) represents the discursive mind and the dot within it, Brahman.

Hindus believe earthly life is cyclical; you are born again and again in a process known as samsara. The quality of these rebirths depends upon your actions (karma) in previous lives. Living a righteous life and fulfilling your duty (dharma) will enhance your chances of being born into a higher caste and better circumstances. Alternatively, if enough bad karma has accumulated rebirth may take animal form. But only as a human can you gain sufficient self-knowledge to escape the cycle of reincarnation and achieve moksha, or liberation. According to some traditions, women are unable to attain moksha. The best they can do is fulfil their dharma and hope for a male incarnation next time round.

Twenty-five-year-old Sakuntala, who recently completed a master's degree, is about to marry 30-year-old Subhashis, an accountant. Sakuntala will leave her parents' home and live with Subhashis in his parents' home, along with his elder brother, his wife and son.

Like the majority of Hindu marriages, this is an arranged marriage; Sakuntala's family selected a husband by using their network of contacts. Sakuntala's parents and her uncles met with Subhashis' family, and each family researched the other to check the prospective couple's suitability, including the compatibility of their horoscopes (an important consideration in the majority of Hindu weddings). After some months, with no impediments found, the decision was made; the wedding day was determined by a priest who advised which were the most auspicious dates and Sakuntala's father sent out the invitations.

There are many ceremonies to be performed before a betrothed couple become partners for life and all take place within the home. Female relatives and friends take turns to ensure that the auspicious sound of a conch shell being blown never ceases during the days of a wedding. The entire neighbourhood is aware that a special event is taking place. Many of these ceremonies are performed to prepare the bride for her new life at her in-laws' home and are carried out under the guidance of the family elders, while the Vedic marriage rituals and ceremonies are conducted by priests (each family has its own priest).

On the day before the wedding day, the bride ceremoniously has her last meal at her father's house as an unmarried woman. She will not eat rice again until she has reached her father-in-law's house the day after the wedding ceremony. The bride (and groom) fast on their wedding day, not eating until after the ceremony.

On the morning of the wedding, the groom's relatives smear turmeric paste on him as part of a ritual cleansing process. They then send the paste to the bride's house. The Vedic rituals begin once it arrives. There is a great flurry of activity as it is smeared on the bride's face and hands. After that it is a free-for-all and turmeric is smeared on anyone who is not quick enough to get out of the way.

A close male relative of the bride accompanies the priest to the room where all the religious ceremonies will take place. They spend the next couple of hours invoking all her ancestors (both paternal and maternal) for the past seven generations, and also invoking gods and goddesses to gain their permission to give the daughter away in marriage. Many offerings, including fruits, vegetables, cereals, honey and flowers, are made by the family as part of the puja.

The bride and groom sit cross-legged on the floor facing the puja trays. The priest sits to one side. The wedding ceremony conducted by the priest lasts for a couple of hours and takes place in the presence of Agni, the god of fire. The bride and groom walk around the fire seven times.

Once the Vedic rituals have been completed, the couple join their family and friends and undergo more rites of passage. The bride is carried on a wooden seat by her brother and his male friends around the groom seven times. The next day, as the bride leaves her home, she throws rice over her shoulder into the folds of her mother's sari, to wish prosperity on the home she is leaving.

The groom tips red vermilion, a sign of marriage, onto the part in his bride's hair.

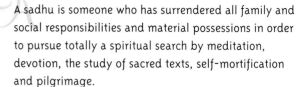

A sadhu is someone who has surrendered all family and social responsibilities and material possessions in order to pursue totally a spiritual search by meditation, devotion, the study of sacred texts, self-mortification and pilgrimage.

A devotee of Shiva, this sadhu has contorted his limbs to such a degree, and for such a long period of time, that the muscle has actually atrophied. Performing austerities such as this is believed to accelerate the attainment of enlightenment, and is not, as it might be considered in the Christian tradition, an act of repentance for past sins.

A wandering sadhu reads the Ramayana (in Hindi) in the Durgiana Temple grounds, Amritsar. (The mark on his forehead is the symbol of Sita, Rama's wife.) When a novice sadhu is initiated into the sadhu brotherhood, his head is completely shaved (if a follower of Shiva; Vaishnavites retain a small tuft), to represent his rebirth. The hair, or jata, is not cut again, unless the sadhu's guru dies. Neither is it groomed, a physical representation of the sadhu's indifference to the ways of the world. It is allowed to grow long and matted, and is usually piled upon the head in a twisted bundle.

Renouncing his name, this sadhu (pictured left) left his family at the age of fifteen. He spent ten years with a guru in Gujarat, from whom he learnt to read and write. Why did he become a sadhu? 'Baghwan ko milne kei lieh' (To meet God). He spends most of his time meditating and reading the Hindu scriptures in which he finds peace and contentment. He believes that meditation is the only way to attain moksha.

He has spent years meditating at sacred sites and temples in Kathmandu, Pashupatinath, Rameswaram, Ayodhya, Jagnathpuri, Dwarka and Varanasi. He intends to go to Jammu next.

SHARAN KAUR

My grandmother sleeps under a large portrait of her husband. The photo formally records the dates of his life and death. Each morning she offers a pranam (respectful salutation) to the portrait. When I visit, I touch my grandmother's feet in a gesture of respect. She acknowledges this with a blessing and then turns to the photograph to make sure my grandfather is included. Since my grandfather's death she has followed the Hindu traditions of widowhood and become vegetarian, worn a white sari and removed most of her jewellery.

SWAPNA MITRA

'As soon as I saw my mother dressed in her wedding clothes, I knew at once that she had made up her mind to commit sati (self-immolation). I started wailing because I realised that I would not only be losing my father, but now my mother as well.'

Manohar Singh was twenty years old when his mother, Thakurani Sugan Kanwar, chose to take her own life after her husband, Brigadier Thakur Zabar Singh, died of a heart attack. 'I remember her telling me in a reassuring tone: "Do not cry, son; it is my time to go".' Although sati had been banned for more than a century, the prohibition failed to stop this Hindu widow from testifying her fierce loyalty by perishing in the flames of her husband's funeral pyre at Jodhpur (Rajasthan) in October 1954. 'We all begged her not to go ahead with it, but she absolutely refused to listen to anyone. She was most anxious that the funeral take place without delay, saying that as time passed, the distance between herself and her husband was growing,' recalls her son. According to Hindu tradition, it is a son's duty to perform the last rites by setting the funeral pyre alight and Manohar Singh, now in his late sixties, still trembles with emotion as he talks about that traumatic moment when he lit the fire. 'It was so painful for me to see my own mother, cradling my dead father's head in her lap, literally melt before my eyes in the orange flames.' Manohar Singh is convinced that his mother was being led by some deep spiritual power, because she did not scream even once as the raging fire enveloped her. 'From the day my mother died, I firmly believe that all of us are guided by some kind of spiritual force. We may not know it or understand it, but it is there.'

SARINA SINGH

Hindus don't only pray to the gods; there is a strong tradition of caring for them. In many Hindu homes there is a thakur ghar, a special place for the gods to live. The gods are generally looked after by the women of the house. Devout Hindus can spend several hours a day worshipping and taking care of the deities that are special to them.

An elderly lady describes her daily puja ritual:

'I do this for the peace of the house and my family. I worship the gods to remove danger. It takes me an hour each day and I do it after I've had my morning bath. All the gods are present in my puja room: Shiva, Durga, Saraswati, Ganesh, Lakshmi and more. I give a namaskar (greeting) to each god. I offer them flowers, tulsi, sandalwood, ganga jal, fruit or sweets and a flower mala (garland) as well as sandalwood paste. Each god has its own mantra, which I recite. Every evening I blow the conch so that the gods will remain in the house.

Another member of her family shows me her statue of Gopal: 'Wherever I go I take Gopal. I carry him with me in my handbag. He is a small baby and he needs a lot of looking after. He's a child and he likes to take sweets.' I noticed that there was a picture of Jesus Christ. 'Oh yes. I bought that picture when I visited Goa. He's a small boy also,' she says with affection.

'I don't have a special room but I've made space for my thakur ghar. There's Lord Krishna, Shiva — all the gods except Lakshmi (the goddess of wealth). She's not there because I don't earn an income,' she says with a laugh.

'Ramakrishna and Vivekananda are also there. I adore them,' she whispers. 'Just as I take care of members of my family, I also look after my gods. I attend to them morning and night. I give them water, flowers and sweets. Any sweets that come into this house are first offered to the gods. During winter I put clothes on them to keep them warm, and at night I place small blankets over them when I put them to bed. At the time of Durga Puja they receive new clothes.'

'If I'm unable to look after my gods, say I'm ill, one of my nieces takes care of them. However, if she also cannot do it, I do it mentally.'

SUSAN MITRA

Mr Ramachandran is a professional parcel packer. At his tiny booth at the Anna Salai Post Office in Chennai, he receives books and other items for packaging. Every morning, before the customers arrive, Mr Ramachandran carefully lays out his tools of trade: his needles and cotton, the white cloth in which he painstakingly wraps the goods, his scissors and the pens with which he diligently inscribes addresses. He then lights some incense and takes ten minutes to bless his tools, his desk and the small space that he leases from the Post Office and his past, as well as future, customers.

'I make my puja to Murugan. I am hoping for a successful day and for all the parcels I make to have a safe journey,' he explains. 'I am a poor man. I cannot travel the world. But, through my job, I meet many people and my parcels travel everywhere from America to Zambia. That gives me much pleasure.'

PETER DAVIS

I am a Hindu. I was born a Hindu. I don't visit temples or follow rituals. I don't believe there is life after death or that all the gods and goddesses that we have can help us live our lives. I do enjoy the revelry and festivals, the paintings, music and sculpture associated with them. The gods and goddesses add great pageantry, colour and detail to our imaginations and their stories made my childhood an enchanted one.

I can't say I am an atheist and I can't say I am a non-practising Hindu. Religion for me is simply following a moral code of life, being compassionate towards and in love with people, animals, nature. I strongly believe in creating good vibrations by positive attitudes and actions. I just carry my religion with me everywhere. I will find moments even in the busiest day to be quiet and meditative. My prayers are directed to the elements around me to protect my children and family from harm, to make us all strong, more loving and caring of each other.

Meera Govil

Most taxi and truck drivers have a small shrine on the dashboard of their vehicles. This taxi driver worships Durga (on the left) and Kali (on the right). The shrine is decorated with fresh flowers and basil leaves daily. Basil, according to Hindus, is sucha, pure.

'Why do you have this shrine in your taxi?'

'Raksha ke lieh' (For protection).

Every Saturday he replaces the lime and chilli decoration and takes the old one to Kalighat Temple where he offers it to the goddess Kali. The lime is believed to 'cut out the evil, bad spirits'.

SHARAN KAUR

What is believed to be India's oldest form of classical dance is found in the country's south. Bharata Natyam remains true to conventions laid down in ancient times. It was originally known as Dasi Attam, a temple art performed by young women called devadasis.

The major theme of the art form is the worship of God through pure devotion and love. The dancer, usually a woman, is a devotee who has been separated from the object of her devotion (God). In her yearning for him, she expresses all the emotions of a tragic heroine mourning for her lover. It takes at least seven years to master the gestures and poses; each and every movement is charged with meaning.

The Kathakali dance form is also based in South India. Although some of its traditions hark back to pre-Hindu times, its present form developed in the seventeenth century when the Raja of Kottarakkara created his own dance troupe to convey the stories of the Ramayana and Mahabharata in the vernacular rather than the more traditional Sanskrit. Only men can become Kathakali dancers. The spectacular make-up and costumes used in Kathakali performances are deeply inscribed with specific symbolic meanings: green-faced characters, for example, are the noble, kingly, divine or heroic types such as Vishnu and Krishna.

Animals, particularly snakes and cows, have been worshipped since ancient times in India. The cow represents fertility and nurturing. The religious protection of cows probably first developed to safeguard them during droughts or famine when they might have been killed off. Cows and large white bulls roam freely in India, even in cities where they can often be seen beside busy roads seemingly unperturbed by the noisy, fume-belching traffic. Nandi, Shiva's bull vehicle, is seen outside Shiva temples.

Elephants have always been sacred in India. As symbols of protection, their sculptured forms uphold massive temple structures and stand guardians at entrances. Within temples their real form greets devotees who willingly place the rupee offering on the trunk tip in return for a blessing.

Snakes, especially cobras, are also considered sacred. Naga stones (snake stones) serve the dual purpose of protecting humans from snakes and propitiating snake gods. Snakes are associated with fertility and welfare.

These rich saffron-coloured flowers are used for garlands, wedding decorations, door decorations and pujas. They are sold both loose and strung together. Each garland has a minimum of thirty-five or thirty-six flowers.

What is their significance? None. Indians love marigolds because of the deep golden orange colour. 'These flowers make the gods happy,' said one flower-seller.

Islam

Islam was founded in Arabia by the Prophet Mohammed in the seventh century AD. The Arabic term islam means to surrender and believers (Muslims) undertake to surrender to the will of Allah (Arabic for God). The will of Allah is revealed in the Koran. God revealed his will to Mohammed, who acted as his messenger.

Prayer books await the faithful.

Islam is monotheistic; God is unique and has no equal or partner. Everything is believed to be created by God and is deemed to have its own place and purpose in the universe. Only God is unlimited and self-sufficient. The purpose of all living things is submission to the divine will. Humans, however, have a choice: whether to obey or disobey. The human weakness is pride, an individual's sense of independence. God never speaks to humans directly, his word is conveyed through messengers — prophets — who are never themselves divine. Mohammed is regarded as the most recent of the prophets, charged with calling people back to God.

All Muslims share a belief in the Five Pillars of Islam: the shahadah or declaration of faith ('there is no god but Allah; Mohammed is his prophet'), which must be recited aloud at least once in a believer's lifetime, with conviction and true understanding; salat or prayer (ideally five times a day and on one's own if one can't make it to a mosque); the zakat or tax which today is usually a voluntary donation in the form of charity; saum or fasting (during the month of Ramadan) for all except the sick, the very young and the elderly and those undertaking arduous journeys; and the hajj or pilgrimage to Mecca, something every Muslim aspires to do at least once.

Islam denies separation between a religious and a secular sphere of life. Its art, therefore, is considered wholly religious. Unlike the rich human figurativeness of Hindu pictorial art, Islam forbids as idolatrous any hint of human imagery. It compensates by having developed the most elaborate and elegant geometric, calligraphic and vegetative designs.

The Jama Masjid or 'Friday Mosque' is where the community gathers for prayer on Friday, Islam's holy day. Smaller, local mosques are used for prayer on other days of the week.

The great Jama Masjid of Old Delhi is both the largest mosque in India and the final architectural extravagance of Emperor Shah Jahan, who was also responsible for the Taj Mahal.

RIGHT
Laying carpets for prayers at the Jama Masjid

LEFT
Twenty-five thousand worshippers can fit into the central courtyard of the Jama Masjid in Old Delhi

Mihrab
The mosque is aligned so that when the faithful pray they are facing towards Mecca; this direction is known as the kibla. Mecca is indicated by the placement of the mihrab, a semicircular space under the central dome, which is reserved for the imam, who leads the prayers.

Mimbar
The mimbar is a seat at the top of the steps at the right of the mihrab, used by the khatib (preacher) during sermons.

Minarets
The minaret is a tower from which the muezzin (crier) calls the faithful to worship.

Southern Gateway
The general public enter by the north or south gate.

Jama Masjid
Delhi

The great mosque of Old Delhi is the largest in India. It was built by Shah Jahan between 1644 and 1658. It has three great gateways, four angle towers and two minarets standing forty metres high. It's constructed of alternating vertical strips of red sandstone and white marble. The mosque functions solely as a place of prayer and teaching. It has no other ceremonial role. Marriages and funerals are conducted in the home.

hern Gateway
general public enter by
orth or south gate.

Central Courtyard
The central courtyard can hold 25,000 people. During Friday prayers and holy festivals, worshippers spill out onto the steps of the mosque.

Ablution Rooms
The mosque is surrounded by several ablution rooms, where wuzoo (ritual washing) is carried out before prayers.

Eastern Gateway
Broad flights of steps lead up to the imposing gateways. The eastern gateway was originally only opened for the emperor, and is now open on Fridays and Muslim festivals.

It is the middle of the day, a Friday, at Delhi's Jama Masjid. The call to prayer booms out from the large speakers at the four entrances to the mosque.

A continuous stream of men files into the mosque. Others place their own mats and face towards Mecca on the steps leading up to the mosque. Most of the men are wearing white caps, some are still to put their caps on, and some of the younger ones wear baseball caps.

It's twenty minutes since the call to prayer began and there are now two rows of men lined up in an orderly manner on the steps leading to the mosque, and countless numbers inside. The men are standing, barefoot, at the end of their mats, all facing Mecca, with their heads bent in prayer. The prayers are broadcast at deafening levels over the loudspeakers. The men's eyes are shut and their arms folded in front of them.

All together they stand bending from their waists, then they kneel down on their mats and each places his forehead on the ground. For the next few minutes they move as one, gracefully, and with perfectly synchronised timing they complete their prayers. A crippled beggar sitting on a wooden board at the base of the steps also participates in the prayers.

It is over: the men quickly stand up and roll up their mats. Many smile as they exchange greetings with their friends. Some of the younger men remove their caps and fix their hair as they walk down the steps and spill out on to the streets of Old Delhi.

SUSAN MITRA

'Every Muslim has to pray five times a day. It's the hukum (command) of Allah.'

The status of women in Islam is possibly one of its most noticeable features. One Koranic verse says, 'Men have authority over women because Allah has made the one superior to the other'.

On the other hand, the Koran also says that women are equal; it is simply that their responsibilities — maintaining the home, providing food, caring for children — are different from those of men. In the modern world, women have gained some independence from the traditional Islamic strictures on women's roles.

LEFT
A young Kashmiri woman reads the Koran on the bare stone floor of the Jama Masjid, Delhi.

RIGHT
A man reads the Koran, Tipu Sultan's Mosque, Kolkata.

For fifty years this man's father was the imam at Tipu Sultan's Mosque in Kolkata (Calcutta). Twelve years ago the community selected him for the role of iman.

'My work is religious: I pray to God. I pray for the public and for all people. Imam means a social worker, particularly for spiritual work. We want good Muslims. By that I mean people who have the right way of speaking and speak well with other castes and religions. People who do better work for the poor and are charitable. People must get along with other castes and religions. I am very happy to do this job. Absolutely, I am an imam.'

SUSAN MITRA

LEFT
The black cap worn by imams symbolises the Holy Ka'aba – the shrine into which is built the black stone given to Ibrahim by Gabriel – enclosed in the Sacred Mosque in Mecca.

RIGHT
Tipu Sultan's Mosque, Kolkata

In Islam, before you pray, you must go through a ritual washing called the wuzoo, which follows a set procedure: your face, your hands and arms up to the elbow, your head and then your feet.

My father used to recount a tale of an old man and a young man at the ablution room of a mosque. The young man saw the old man carrying out wuzoo in the wrong order. Instead of telling him that he was doing something wrong, he asked the old man to show him how to wuzoo. The older man showed him — incorrectly. The younger man thanked him and said nothing else, but his request had jolted the older man into thought. He wanted to make sure that the procedure was indeed as he had demonstrated. On checking he realised his mistake; the next time he saw the young man at the mosque he called him aside and set him straight.

Learning respect for one's elders is a part of all religions, including Islam, but I think my father had a particularly clever way of revealing how to correct one's elders without showing loss of respect for them.

Masood Hayat

When I was a boy of seven or eight my parents organised a moulana, or religious teacher for me, who taught me to read the Koran and gave me lessons on Islam.

The moulana demonstrated the differences between Islam and other religions in many ways. One of his favourite methods was to use 'what if' stories, and the one that I remember best was when he asked me to imagine that my father had died that day.

How would a mourner from the West greet me?

By saying, 'Good morning'.

How would a mourner who was Muslim greet me?

By saying, 'Salaam Alaikum' (May God be with you).

'Which response,' the moulana wanted to know, 'is more appropriate on the day of your father's death? Can it really be a "good morning"?'

I suspected then that this was his method of mild indoctrination. Now I can see in some of the moulana's strategies a mixture of the hard practicality of the West and the delicate etiquette of the East.

MASOOD HAYAT

Ramadan, the month of fasting, is greeted with a sense of challenge. Those fasting are reminded of those less fortunate than themselves; fasting builds discipline and willpower.

A Muslim explains what the month of fasting means to him:

'The idea is not to let any food, drink or smoke enter your body during the hours between sunrise and sundown. I unintentionally broke my fast on two occasions; hunger does funny things to a young mind. There was a great sense of guilt. I felt better when I told my mother and she explained that there was no sin in unintentionally breaking a fast. I was to try harder next time.

At sunrise those members of the family fasting would have a fairly substantial breakfast. At sundown the breaking of the fast would be celebrated with a feast: unleavened bread, rice, meat and vegetable curries washed down with rose-hip cordial or lassi, a milk and yogurt drink. This was followed by an extensive range of your favourite sweetmeats. Yum!'

Masood Hayat

An imam explains what Ramadan means to him:

'We observe Ramadan because it is the order of God. For all Muslims, Ramadan is your duty.' He pauses for a slight moment and says softly, 'You must complete your duty. Every religion has its own period of fasting, its own version of Ramadan. If I don't complete one day of Ramadan there will be punishment. I'm very happy when I complete Ramadan. Spiritual power shines.'

Susan Mitra

Meena cleans eleven houses each day. It is now close to noon and she's cheerful and working hard. Meena hasn't eaten or drunk anything, not even a drop of water, since 4.30 this morning.

Eid-ul-Fitr is the Islamic festival that celebrates the ending of the month of fasting, Ramadan. After morning prayers, there is a family lunch: lots of food and a traditional vermicelli sweet: sheer korma. Then presents for the children, sometimes in the form of money, called eidy. Visits in the late afternoon to friends and family. More food, more sheer korma, more eidy.

MASOOD HAYAT

THIS PAGE
Muslim vendors on Rabindra Sarani Road, near the Nakhoda Mosque in Kolkata, sell dried fruit, dates, raisins, dried coconuts and vermicelli.

PREVIOUS AND FACING PAGE
Popular Eid-ul-Fitr festival food: dates and vermicelli noodles

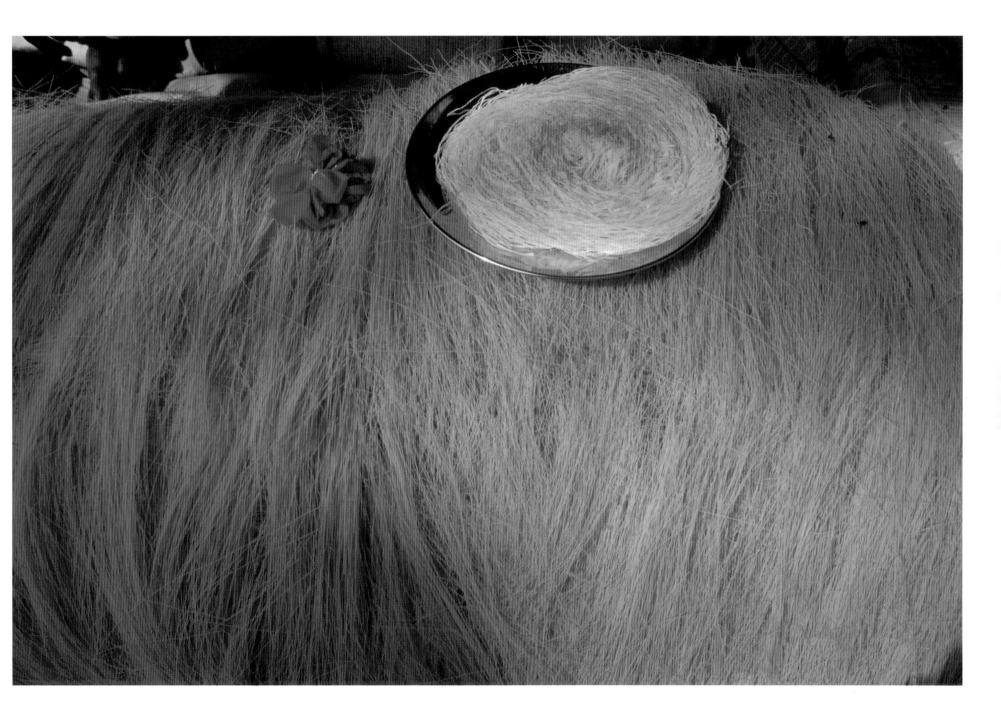

Sikhism

There are some 16 million Sikhs in India and most come from the Punjab, where the Sikh religion was founded by Guru Nanak in the late fifteenth century. Sikhism began as a reaction against the caste system and the Brahmin domination of ritual. It was conceived at a time of great social unrest and was an attempt to fuse the best of Islam and Hinduism.

Sikhism also accords women equal status with men. Like other attempts at equality, there are problems putting this into practice.

Sikhs believe in one god and reject the worship of idols. Like Hindus and Buddhists, they accept the cycle of birth, death and rebirth and karma, as well as the notion that only a human birth offers the chance for salvation. There is no ascetic or monastic tradition for ending the eternal cycles of death and rebirth in Sikhism.

Sikhs suffered persecution for two centuries at the hands of conquerors, particularly under the Muslim rulers. In 1606, Guru Arjan, the fifth guru, was tortured and he became the first of many Sikh martyrs. After his death the sixth guru formalised the fusion of religion and secular power and made it an important part of the Sikh religion.

On 13 April 1699, in Anandpur, Guru Gobind Singh baptised five of his followers who came from different castes and founded the Khalsa, or 'the pure' — a sacred military brotherhood. He made them drink amrit (nectar) from a common bowl and gave them the surname of Singh.

Golden Temple, Amritsar (also previous and following pages)

The Granth Sahib (the Sikh holy book) contains the teachings of the ten Sikh gurus as well as those of learned Hindu and Muslim saints, who lived at different times and belonged to different castes. The holy scriptures, arranged in poetic verses, are the only object of worship in gurudwaras (temples) or in Sikh homes. The teachings are central to Sikhism. The holy Granth Sahib was compiled by the fifth guru, Guru Arjan, in 1604.

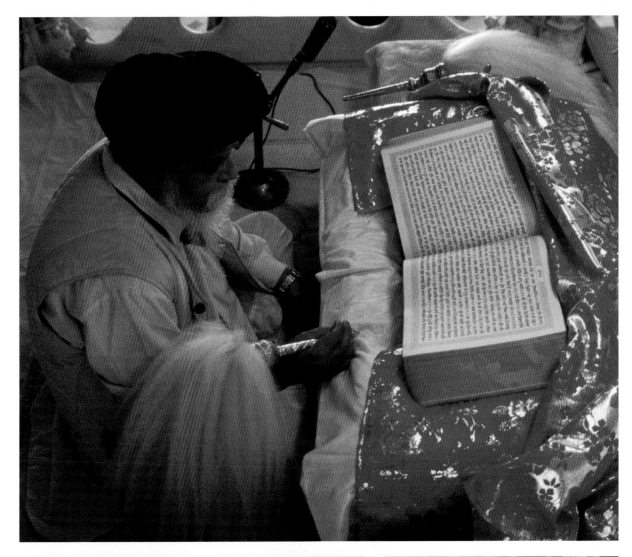

ABOVE RIGHT
Priest reading the Granth Sahib, Bherra Gurudwara, Kolkata

RIGHT
Worshippers at the Golden Temple, Amritsar

Ajit Singh was born in Amritsar and has been coming to the Golden Temple every day since he was a small boy. 'First thing each morning I read the holy book for two hours. I do this before I eat anything. The main aim of our religion is for us to achieve peace of mind at the time of death. This body will die but the mind will remain alive. It is necessary to win over the mind before death and keep it under control. It's easier to win the whole world than to win the mind. It's not a simple affair, it takes a lot of concentrated effort. I want to achieve mental peace.'

SUSAN MITRA

The Nishan Sahib is the Sikh flag and every gurudwara has one installed on a high site in the temple grounds.

Pilgrim Accommodation
Hospitality is provided free to travellers and pilgrims in four hundred basic rooms, with ablutions performed at washbasins in the central courtyard.

Gurudwara Baba Atal
This late-eighteenth-century tower, nine storeys high, was built in memory of a nine-year-old boy who was honoured with the title of Baba due to his precocious wisdom.

Hari Mandir
The Hari Mandir, also known as the Darbar Sahib, is the most sacred part of the temple complex. It is a two-storeyed marble structure with gold-plated domes and semi-precious stone-encrusted walls. The golden dome, said to be gilded with 100kg of pure gold, represents an inverted lotus flower, turned back to earth to symbolise the Sikhs' concern with the problems of this world. The Hari Mandir enshrines the holy book, the Granth Sahib. No formal rituals are conducted here, but hymns are sung throughout the day and night.

Guru-ka-Langar
Approximately thirty-five thousand people are fed here daily. People from all walks of life, irrespective of colour, caste and creed, are welcomed; all sit on the floor and eat together.

Central Sikh Museum
A gallery of Sikh gurus, saints and warriors

Main Entrance & Clock Tower

Central Sikh Museum
A gallery of Sikh gurus, saints and warriors

Parkarma
Pilgrims use this marble walkway, which surrounds the Sarowar, or sacred pool, to circumambulate the Hari Mandir.

GOLDEN TEMPLE
AMRITSAR, PUNJAB

According to tradition, the Buddha is believed to have journeyed through this region and remarked upon the suitability of the secluded site as one in which salvation could be attained. Guru Nanak, the founder of Sikhism, was also charmed by the site, and in the late sixteenth century a natural pool here was enlarged and named Amrit Sarowar — Pool of Nectar. The city derives its name from this pool, at the heart of the temple complex, in which Sikh pilgrims bathe.

Gurus' Bridge
Pilgrims walk along this causeway to reach the Hari Mandir. The sacred Granth Sahib is ceremoniously carried along the causeway each morning from the Akal Takht and installed in the Hari Mandir; it is carried back along the causeway to the Akal Takht each evening.

Nishan Sahib
These Sikh flags are hoisted in the temple grounds and can be seen at all Sikh gurudwaras.

Akal Takht
Built in 1609, this is the seat of secular power, where the Sikh parliament meets.

K. HAMBLET '99

My father was a granthi (priest) in a small town in Malaysia. My mother made sure that we were models for the other children in the community. We recited prayers in the morning, evening and night and went to the gurudwara every Sunday. There was no escaping it. My brothers sang shabads (hymns) at home and in the gurudwara. Whenever my mother had to discipline us, she had an amazing ability to pluck suitable verses from the Granth Sahib to support her viewpoint.

As I matured and steeped myself in the 'sophistication' of Western living, I started to question aspects of the Indian culture, my blind faith and conformity. I still went to the gurudwara. I still sang. But I wanted to be a modern woman, to be different, from my mother, my roots. Just a little…

A pilgrimage to the holiest Sikh shrine, the Golden Temple at Amritsar, was still something I wanted to do. Finally, I had the opportunity to go. I didn't know what to expect but I had to see it for myself.

Leaving behind me the street life of Amritsar, the chaos and traffic madness of cows and rickshaws, I entered the temple grounds, left my shoes with sewadaars (volunteers), covered my head with my dupatta (scarf) and dipped my feet in the warm water flowing in shallow troughs at the temple entrance.

I stood on the parkarma, the marble walkway, and suddenly there it was. Glowing, living, a majestic presence rising from the centre of the sacred pool.

The marble floor was smooth and clean beneath my feet, unlike most of the other places I had visited. Despite the fact that around fifty thousand people visit this temple daily, there was no pushing and shoving. No-one asking for donations. Order and

organisation…in India? I had only seen chaos until now.

Volunteers stood in a corner with cups of water for weary pilgrims and visitors. In the kitchen, others sat in rows peeling potatoes, cooking and serving food. People were here not just to see and receive but to give. The place was alive and charged with energy. For Sikhs, it is a privilege to have the opportunity to do sewa (voluntary service). Giving was everywhere.

I entered the temple proper, placed a donation and then knelt before the Granth Sahib, my forehead touching the floor. The granthi sat fanning the Granth Sahib with a whisk. I stopped briefly to listen to the raagis (musicians) and their soft, melodious kirtan (hymn-singing). The sangat (congregation of worshippers) sat silent on the floor, motionless in devotion.

I went upstairs and walked around, reading the excerpts from the holy scriptures inscribed in gold on the walls, entranced by the sheer beauty of the place. In awe. Lightly touching the jewel- and semiprecious-stone-studded walls, the intricate designs and flower motifs carved in gold. Something was happening. This could not be real. The walls were singing a beautiful shabad — to me.

Tuun kaheh doleh prania, tudh rakhega sirjan har Jin paida is tuun kiya, soyi dei adhaar.

Why do you waver, hesitate? You are protected by the Almighty God. He who created you will give you solace, comfort.

Where had I heard those words before? From my mother, of course. Now they came back to me and embraced me.

The veneer of Western sophistication was stripped off me. I stood in the presence of something powerful, beautiful, indescribable. It shook me. Overwhelmed, I wept.

I remembered my mother saying to me: 'I would love to spend my last days in the shadows of the Golden Temple.' I now knew why.

My pilgrimage was complete. I had not asked for anything but I was walking away with a gift. I left with the shabad resonating in my soul.
    Tuun kaheh doleh prania, tudh rakhega sirjan har…

Sharan Kaur

FOLLOWING PAGES
A local volunteer says he has been taking part in the washing of the parkarma since the age of fifteen. 'It's only with the grace of God that you can do this sewa. Look at that old woman over there – bending and cleaning. It's hard work. But sewa is one way of meeting God. Moreover this work keeps me physically and mentally fit.'

It is the wish of most Sikhs to visit the Golden Temple and bathe in the sarowar (sacred pool) at least once in their lifetime. Some believe that bathing in the sacred waters will wash away their sins or cure them of all ailments.

In 1984 the Indian Army, under orders from Prime Minister Indira Gandhi, stormed the Golden Temple and killed the Sikh fundamentalist Sant Bhindrawale and others. Bhindrawale and his armed followers had based themselves in the temple and were campaigning for a separate Sikh state — Khalistan. The subsequent assassination of Indira Gandhi by two of her Sikh bodyguards and the reprisal killings of thousands of Sikhs severely damaged relations between Sikhs and the government.

The Indian government repaired some of the damage done to the temple but the Sikhs tore it down. They wanted to rebuild it with their own hands. Artisans and volunteers worked day and night at the temple, beating gold leaves on to copper sheets, to repair the damage. Twenty-four layers of gold leaf were used for the gilding.

Volunteers at the Golden Temple cook chapatis (unleavened wholemeal bread), rolling them out and cooking them on a huge griddle. Others prepare kheer (a dessert), boil gallons of milk, and cook dhal and vegetables in huge cauldrons.

At most gurudwaras, visitors and worshippers are fed daily in the afternoons and evenings. No-one who requests food and drink is turned away. The temple kitchen-cum-eating-place is known as the Guru-ka-Langar and it is run by volunteers, most of whom are pilgrims themselves. Guru Nanak, the first guru of the Sikhs, disapproved of the Hindu caste system and introduced the practice of 'breaking bread' together, allowing all people, irrespective of colour, caste and creed, to sit and eat together. Guru Nanak preached: 'Kirat karo, nam japo, wand shako' (Work hard, recite the name of God, and share with the less fortunate).

Wich dunia sew kemaieh, taan dargaih baisan paiyeh.

Earn merit by doing service in this world, to reap rewards in heaven.

Sikhs are the most visible religious group in India because of the symbols they wear. The five kakkars were introduced by Guru Gobind Singh to denote the Khalsa brotherhood.

The karra is a steel bangle, worn on the right wrist, which symbolises strength – some say fearlessness. The kaccha are loose underpants that symbolise modesty. The kangha is a comb with which to maintain the ritually uncut hair. The kesh is the unshaven beard and uncut hair that symbolise saintliness. The kirpan is a sabre or sword, carried at all times, which symbolises power and dignity, to be used only in self-defence or to uphold justice: 'When all other means have failed, it is righteous to draw the sword' (Guru Gobind Singh).

Rajbarinder Singh, a 22-year-old Sikh, in Ludhiana, Punjab, reads scriptures from the Granth Sahib in his home. 'I don't think I would have been religious had I not been born a Sikh. I don't know why I feel this. It feels so good when I recite the Gurbani (holy scriptures). If one follows the Gurbani I don't think one will suffer in life. The holy book in 1428 pages has everything that I need to know. My religion is only five hundred years old but there is so much in it that I feel proud that I am a Sikh.'

Most devout Sikhs have a place in their homes in which the Granth Sahib is kept. It is installed in the centre of the room on a platform overlaid with clean cloth with a colourful canopy above it. The holy book is wrapped in embroidered cloth. It is treated with great reverence and ceremoniously opened in the morning. The holy scriptures are read during the day and are wrapped and put to rest after sunset prayers. Sikhs recite their daily prayers in the morning, evening and at night.

Although the Sikhs do not believe in idol worship some Sikhs have pictures of the ten gurus in their homes as a point of focus.

The kirpan is one of the five kakkars (symbols worn by members of the Sikh brotherhood). This dagger is carried at all times and symbolises power and dignity.

Sikhs do not believe in ancestor worship but Sikhism's strong links with Hinduism emerge at village level. Sikh cultural life overlaps with that of the Hindus in many ways.

Some villages in the Punjab have a samadhi, a sacred shrine built in the memory of a highly respected ancestor. This samadhi was built in memory of Baba Anokh Singh, seven generations ago. Villagers, like this young woman opposite, pray at the shrine on special occasions such as the birth of a child or if a wish has been fulfilled. This is reminiscent of puja at Hindu shrines.

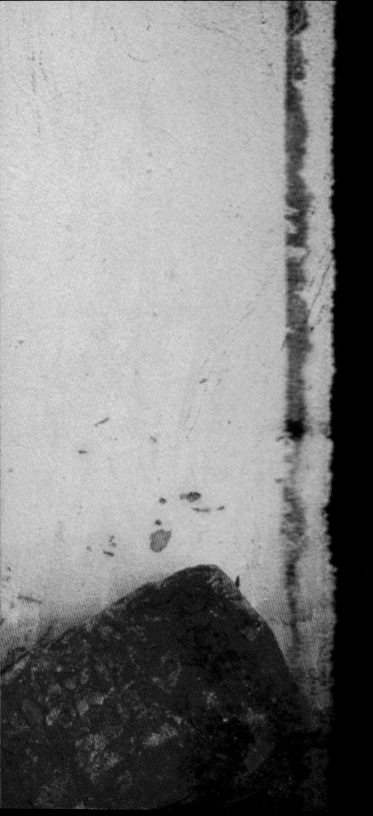

Around six million people practise Buddhism in India, fewer than either Christianity or Sikhism. The Buddha (Awakened One) was a historical figure who is generally believed to have lived from about 563 to 483 BC. Formerly a prince (Siddhartha Gautama), the Buddha, at the age of twenty-nine, embarked on a quest for enlightenment and relief from the world of suffering. He finally achieved the state of full awareness (nirvana) at Bodhgaya, aged thirty-five. Critical of the caste system, dependence upon Brahmin priests and the unthinking worship of gods, the Buddha urged his disciples to seek truth within their own experiences.

Prayer flags above Leh in Ladakh. These coloured flags (red, blue, yellow, white and green) are an efficient way to distribute prayers. The prayers are carried by the wind straight to the ears of the gods. Strings of tattered prayer flags are often seen at high mountain passes, left there by travellers to facilitate a safe journey.

Buddha taught that existence is based on four noble truths: life is rooted in suffering; suffering is caused by craving; one can find release from suffering by eliminating craving; and the way to eliminate craving is by following the Eight-Fold Path. This path consists of: right understanding; right intention; right speech; right action; right livelihood; right effort; right awareness; and right concentration. By successfully complying with these things one can attain nirvana.

In the centuries after the Buddha's death, Buddhism split into many sects, of which there remain two main groups: Theravada and Mahayana. Theravada means 'the word of the elders' — they believe that the teachings of the Buddha should be preserved and practised in their original forms. Mahayana means 'the great vehicle' — they believe that the teachings can be adapted to time and place, making the attainment of enlightenment more accessible to lay people.

The rise of Buddhism inspired some of India's greatest art, evident for example in the rock-cut caves of Ellora, the cave paintings of Ajanta and the exquisitely carved sculpture of Sanchi.

Buddhism had virtually died out in most of India by the start of the twentieth century. It enjoyed something of a revival from the 1950s onward among intellectuals and Dalits, India's so-called Untouchables, who were disillusioned with the caste system. The number of followers has been further boosted with the influx of Tibetan refugees and the 1975 annexation of the previously independent kingdom of Sikkim. Ladakhi Buddhists follow traditions similar to those found in Tibet.

ABOVE LEFT
This painting at Pemayangtse Gompa, Sikkim, depicts Chenmizang, a Lokapala, or one of the Guardian Kings who guard the four cardinal points. Chenmizang is the Guardian King of the West. The Lokapala protect the universe and the heavens against the outer demons, and are always found in the vestibules of gompas (monasteries) in Sikkim. Chenmizang is the king of the nagas, or snake spirits, and a snake can be seen coiled around his left hand. In his right hand he holds a stupa.

LEFT
A monk lights butter lamps at Bodhgaya, one of the most important places of pilgrimage for Buddhists, as it was here that the Buddha attained enlightenment whilst meditating under a bodhi tree.

ABOVE
Monks in full ceremonial costume prepare to perform a chaam, or lama dance.

RIGHT
Prayer books at a gompa in Sikkim

On top of a squat hill rising from the central Indian plains stands the country's finest Buddhist architecture, and some of the most important reminders of the rise of Buddhism in India. Buddhism's most famous convert, the Emperor Ashoka, built the first stupas (monuments containing relics of the Buddha or Buddhist monks) on top of the hill of Sanchi in the third century BC. Many stupas and other religious structures were added over the succeeding centuries.

As Buddhism was gradually replaced by Hinduism in its land of origin, the site decayed and was eventually forgotten. Since its rediscovery in 1818 it has been carefully repaired and restored. Today Sanchi is one of the most evocative places in India.

The western torana of the Great Stupa features some of the finest and liveliest sculptures at Sanchi. As the Buddha could not be represented directly in art at this time, he appears in various forms, including a bodhi tree, a wheel, an elephant and even a stupa.

There are five main stupas at Sanchi, surrounded by a surreal scattering of ruined temples, pillars and monasteries. The pinnacle of the architecture here is the Great Stupa, a plain dome-shaped structure in itself, with four superbly carved toranas (gateways) arranged around its perimeter. These toranas, erected around 35 BC, are like an intricately carved book on the life of the Buddha. They depict stories from the Jatakas (episodes from the Buddha's past lives).

Temple & Monastery
This monastery was in a commanding position at the edge of the hilltop, with the conventional plan of cells arranged around a courtyard. The adjacent temple was surrounded on three sides by a processional path. The image of the Buddha discovered here seems to have been installed at a later date, as it did not quite fit the plinth on which it was mounted. It represents the Buddha in a seated position in the earth-touching attitude (bhumisparsa mudra).

Great Stupa
This is the main structure on the hill at Sanchi. It was built by the emperor Ashoka in the third century BC to enshrine relics of the Buddha. The construction of stupas was believed to acquire great spiritual merit for the builder.

This fifth-century temple is fronted by a porch supported by pillars bearing lion capitals.

Stupa Three
This stupa was built shortly after the Great Stupa, and has only one torana, or gateway. It contained caskets in which were the relics of two important disciples of the Buddha.

Northern Torana
This is the best preserved of the gateways, or toranas. Scenes carved on the gateway include a monkey offering a bowl of honey to the Buddha.

Processional Path
This processional path was used by monks and lay people to circumambulate the stupa. It was accessed by a flight of stairs, known as a sopana, on the south side of the stupa.

Processional Path
Pilgrims circumambulated the stupa along this path (behind the balustrade), as with all Buddhist monuments, in a clockwise direction, keeping the stupa to their right.

Balustrade
This balustrade, or vedika, encompasses the stupa. Its component parts were donated by pilgrims, whose names are inscribed on the masonry.

Southern Torana
This is the oldest of the four gateways. The elaborate carvings include scenes of the Buddha's birth and also events from Ashoka's life as a Buddhist.

This seventh-century temple once enshrined a small stupa which contained a casket housing relics.

Great Temple
The stone plinth is all that remains of this enormous temple, which originally had a wooden superstructure which burnt down centuries ago.

Unlike some of the other important Buddhist sites in India, Sanchi had no direct connection with the life of the Buddha. The secluded hilltop was selected as a place of pilgrimage due to its proximity to Vidisa, an important city from which the emperor Ashoka selected a wife. Sanchi was close enough to the city to attract local pilgrims, but was far enough away to provide a place of peace and reflection for the monks and nuns who lived at the site.

Monasteries
Monks and nuns lived in these viharas in cells that surrounded a central courtyard. The monasteries all date from the medieval period.

Ashoka Column
Following his conversion to Buddhism in 262 BC, Ashoka assembled pillars across the breadth of his enormous empire on which were inscribed edicts propounding Buddhist principles. The inscription on the fragments of the Ashoka column at Sanchi exhorts his people not to create schisms in the Buddhist fold. The edict was to hold sway 'for as long as the Moon and the Sun shall endure'. The column was surmounted by a capital, bearing four back-to-back lions, which now forms the state emblem of India, and can be seen on every bank note.

This monastery contained 22 cells around a central courtyard.

K. HAMBLET

I spent six months in Dharamsala. Each day I spent an hour with three young Tibetan monks — Lobsang, Tsephel and Thupten — who were keen to further their English skills. Abstract nouns proved difficult, but it was these that the monks were so interested in: love, peace, hate. How do you encapsulate the concept of love for three Tibetan Buddhist monks? Finally Lobsang slapped his thighs and laughed his understanding. 'Ah, Love. Dalai Lama!'

One day we came across the word 'wish' in a reader. I tried to explain the concept of desiring something. 'Wish means to hope for,' I ventured. 'There must be something you wish for.' Three blank faces stared back at me. After a prolonged silence Tsephel offered hesitantly, 'I wish long life for the Dalai Lama'. Round, jolly Lobsang countered with: 'I wish long life for my father and mother'. Thupten, catching on, wished for 'a free Tibet'.

Hundreds of Westerners visit Dharamsala every year, searching — wishing — for peace of mind. Yet not one of those three young men wished for anything for himself.

MICHELLE COXALL

PREVIOUS PAGE
Lamayuru Gompa, Ladakh

LEFT
Monk performing puja

TOP RIGHT
Novice monks at lessons, Darjeeling

BOTTOM RIGHT
Novice monks at breakfast, Pemayangtse Gompa, Sikkim

Monks preparing food and playing a
popular board game called carrom

Other Religions

CHRISTIANITY

When the Portuguese explorer Vasco da Gama dropped anchor at Calicut (Kozhikode in present day Kerala) in 1498 he claimed to be seeking Christians and spices. He found both.

Christianity is said to have arrived in South India (specifically the Malabar Coast) with the Apostle St Thomas in AD 52. Scholars believe that it is more likely that Christianity arrived around the fourth century with a Syrian merchant (Thomas Cana) who set out for Kerala with four hundred families. Catholicism established a strong presence in South India in the wake of Vasco da Gama's visit in 1498. Catholic sects that have been active in the region include the Dominicans, Franciscans and Jesuits.

Protestantism arrived with the English, the Dutch and the Danish, and their legacy lives on today in the Church of South India.

India has about 18 million Christians, some three-quarters of whom are in South India.

Church of St Francis, Old Goa

Conversion to Christianity from Hinduism has perhaps always existed (as it has to Islam and Buddhism) but, overall, in small numbers. Invariably converts come from among the poorest and most oppressed Hindus attempting to escape the strictures of the caste system. Ironically, and not surprisingly, a form of caste has developed within both Christianity and Islam as well.

Religious art inside Christian churches often has a Hindu decorative quality about it: bold, colourful and clearly popular. Only the images are different.

FAR LEFT
St Paul's Cathedral, Kolkata

LEFT
Nativity scene, Goa

ABOVE
Christian auto-rickshaw

'When you enter a church there's a pin-drop silence and sometimes that silence overwhelms you,' says Mr Gervasio Mascarenhas, as I wait to speak with Panaji's head parish priest, Father Santana Carvalho.

Father Carvalho is a busy man. He presides over one of Goa's largest active churches, the magnificent church of Our Lady of the Immaculate Conception in the state's relaxed capital city of Panaji. The gleaming whitewashed façade of the church is reached by a series of criss-crossing steps. Consecrated in 1541, it was here that Portuguese sailors would give thanks for a safe voyage.

'The church is full to overflowing every Sunday,' says Father Carvalho, 'and there are services given every day in Konkani (the Goan language), Portuguese and English. People come to the church with much love.' He adds that the entire Roman Catholic population attends church at least once a week. 'In public life the Christians are united and form themselves in communities.' Regular church attendance and Goa's myriad religious festivals reinforce this unity: pulling together the local communities in a celebration of their faith.

Goa's Roman Catholics make up somewhere between twenty-five and thirty-three per cent of the total state population — Hinduism is still the predominant religion — but Father Carvalho describes the situation in Goa as one of complete religious tolerance. 'Hindus and Catholics respect each other's beliefs. There is absolute tolerance in Goa.'

PAUL HARDING

LEFT
Church of Our Lady of the Immaculate Conception,
Panaji, Goa

St Paul's Anglican Cathedral in Kolkata (Calcutta) was built in
1847 and features a large collection of mosaic panels. The
stained glass work here is beautiful. A massive restoration
program was undertaken recently and 40 lakhs (about
US$100,000) was raised. Most of the money came from local
people. Father Noel Sen, the senior priest, has been at this
church for more than fifty years. 'I've been here since Sunday
school,' he smiled.

The caretaker, GP Loxton, an Anglo-Indian originally from the
West Indies, settled in Kolkata in 1939. A Roman Catholic, he
sees no difference between Catholics and Protestants. He takes
communion every Sunday. 'It makes me feel alive.'

LEFT
Puttanpalli Church at Thrissur with Christmas decoration.
This church exists in a city which is centred on the enormous
Vadakkunathan Kshetram Hindu temple, one of the largest
Hindu temples in Kerala.

GURUS AND ASHRAMS

'Guru' traditionally means either 'the dispeller of darkness' or 'heavy with wisdom', and thousands visit India each year to receive darshan, an audience with a guru (literally, 'a glimpse of God').

Most gurus live in an ashram (a place of striving), a reflection of the Hindu belief that life is a continuous struggle through a series of reincarnations that eventually leads to spiritual salvation. Any place of striving where like-minded people gather to explore their spirituality can be called an ashram, be it a commercial complex or an individual's home. An ashram is established when a guru stays in one place and disciples congregate around him or her, in time buying land, building facilities and making donations. The ashrams of Ramakrishna in Kolkata, Sai Baba in Puttaparthi and Osho in Pune are among the best known.

Many ashrams have codes of conduct, which can include daily bathing and avoiding unnecessary speech, vegetarianism and abstinence from eggs, tobacco, alcohol, garlic and onions. Most people in ashrams wear white, the colour of purity.

A devotee of Sai Baba studies a picture of the revered guru.

While visiting the Durgiana Temple in Amritsar, I met Mr Ghai. He started talking to me and produced some Sai Baba literature. He was bursting to tell me about Sai Baba.

'Bhagwan Shri Satya Sai Baba is an incarnation of God. I follow him because he does so many miracles which ordinary people cannot do. He can make cancer cancel.

I previously worshipped Lord Krishna but he's physically not on this earth. Somebody told me about Shri Baba. He told me Sai Baba is a living god so I went to see him, and I started worshipping Krishna and Sai Baba. I had the opportunity to have an interview with Sai Baba. I had only one wish. I asked that God give me his devotion. When my turn came, Sai Baba asked me, "Do you worship anybody?" I replied, "Krishna". Sai Baba created a small Lord Krishna in his palm and gave it to me. It was a matter of great surprise to me — a small baby Krishna which I keep in my own temple. It's very beautiful. The Krishna statue is made of metal but to me it's more valuable than gold.

You can't go anywhere on this earth and find a living god but Sai Baba is a living god.'

Susan Mitra

JAINISM

Jainism, which today has about three million followers in India, was founded in the sixth century BC by Mahavira, a contemporary of the Buddha. Jains believe that only by achieving complete purity of the soul can one attain liberation. Purity means shedding all karman — matter generated by one's actions — which binds itself to the soul. By following various austerities (such as fasting, meditation, retreating to lonely places) one can shed karman and purify the soul. Right conduct is essential, and can really only be fully realised by the monk as opposed to the ordinary person. Fundamental to the right mode of conduct for monks and laity is ahimsa (non-violence) in thought and in deed.

ABOVE
Sandalwood paste and flowers for adorning the gods

RIGHT
A brass idol of the Gomateshvara statue dwarfed by the mighty stone foot of the statue itself, Sravanabelagola, Karnataka. Carved from a single rock, this immense image depicts Bahubali, who gained liberation of the soul by renouncing the material world and meditating while standing bolt upright in the forest.

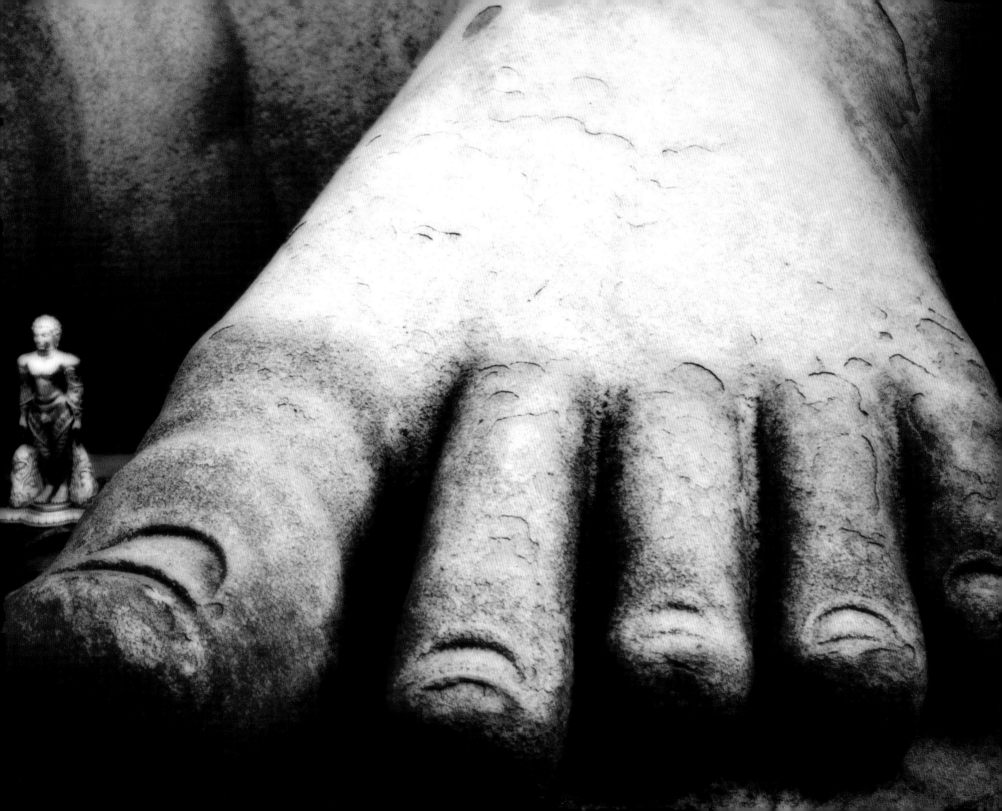

The religious disciplines of the laity are less severe than for monks. Some Jain monks go naked and use the palms of their hands as begging bowls. The slightly less ascetic maintain a bare minimum of possessions including a broom with which they sweep the path before them to avoid stepping on any living thing and a piece of cloth which is tied over the mouth to prevent accidentally inhaling insects.

A lone Jain monk prays to the giant Gomateshvara statue on Indragiri Hill, Sravanabelagola. He wears virtually no clothing and clutches a string of beads and a pinchi (or morpicchi), a whiskbroom made from peacock feathers.

Shrine to a deity in Swetamber Dadjis temple and garden complex, Kolkata

Jain temples — with the distinctive red-and-white striped banner flying from the top — are among the finest in India. The Jain community is a wealthy one and believes in spending money maintaining, improving, (often 'modernising') and cleaning (spotlessly so) their places of devotion. Mornings are the time for quiet devotion. Evening may produce music, singing, at times spontaneous dancing. Devotees, dressed in their best, leave calm and at peace — as is the intention.

Often painted over the doors of houses, the swastika is an ancient symbol sacred to Jains, Hindus and Buddhists that is believed to bring good luck. The bent crossbars symbolise motion. Left-facing crossbars have a negative connotation.

RIGHT
Jain devotees sweep the floor of an exquisite marble temple at Ranakpur, Rajasthan.

LEFT
White marble is the main construction material of Jain temples. Intricate designs and symbols such as swastikas feature on walls and columns. Colourful enamel and stone inlays can also be seen on walls and ceilings.

JUDAISM

There may be no more than 17,000 Jews left in India but the community is an ancient one. Jews arrived in Kochi, an island in the modern state of Kerala, in the sixth century BC and for a long time flourished there. The Kochi synagogue has now only a handful of worshippers left in its congregation, because the attraction of emigration to Israel has in recent times dissipated the community.

Late on a Friday afternoon the 38-degree Kolkata heat had taken its toll, and I decided to buy some bread for a snack. I saw a sign for a bakery and stepped inside.

To my surprise, as I looked along the shelves, I discovered not one, but eight, perfectly made challot, a plaited bread that Jews traditionally eat at Sabbath meals. Further browsing turned up such classic middle-European Jewish baked goods as a shelf of bagels, a tray of mandelbrod (almond bread) and a cake that looked remarkably like my grandmother's world-famous kugelhoff.

'You, where are you from?'

The question had come from the rear of the bakery, where three Indian men were seated behind a counter, sipping tea. I replied cautiously. 'Australia.'

'No, no, no. Where are your parents from?'

'Well, my mother is South African originally, and my father is from Israel.'

'Ah, I thought so. Shalom shalom. Ma'shlomcha. Welcome to my shop. You'll see that my bread is very tasty. The best challot in India.'

Nahoum's bakery has been owned and operated for more than fifty years by a Kolkata Jewish family. The present owner, David, told me that while most Jews had left Kolkata for Israel, England and even Australia, his family had stayed. He reckoned that there were around a hundred Jews still living in the city. He said proudly, 'As long as there is one Jew, I'll continue to make challot on Friday. It is tradition.'

EYTAN ULIEL

The front door of the synagogue was shut, so I knocked. After a few moments it opened. 'The synagogue is closed until next week,' a young man with a moustache informed me curtly. He began closing the door, so I had to be quick:

'Look, I'm a Jew, I want to come in for the Pesach prayer service.' My use of the Hebrew word for Passover had some effect, and the man at the door paused and looked at me closely. 'How do I know you're Jewish?'

I recited the first few lines of the She'ma, one of the few Jewish prayers I know by heart. The man at the door opened it just wide enough to let me in and beckoned me to enter.

There were only nine, mostly elderly, men in the synagogue that evening, so my appearance meant that there was a minyan (the quorum necessary for a full Jewish prayer service).

This was, according to the synagogue guardian, Len, an increasingly rare event, although he told me proudly that there had been more than twenty people present for the first night of the Passover holiday and last year they had celebrated a bar mitzvah in the synagogue. I sat quietly on a bench at the side of the synagogue, participating in the prayers.

I introduced myself and chatted with the last remnants of what was once a thriving community. Len told me that today there are fewer than thirty Jews left in Kochi, but that their sense of Jewish identity is still strong.

Even though in fifty years there may be no more Jews in Kochi, for me, at least, they will always be there — frail old men walking home from synagogue along Jew Street on a hot Indian Friday night.

Eytan Uliel

For all of their fifty-five married years Sarah Cohen (70) and Jacob Cohen (80) have lived in the same house on Jew Street, just two hundred metres from the 430-year-old synagogue in Kochi, Kerala. They are the oldest members of the dwindling Jewish community. 'I was born in this house,' says Jacob, a retired journalist and lawyer. 'Most people from here have gone to Israel but this is where I will die.'

Jacob has traced five generations of his family in India. 'Originally my people were from Iraq. When they were expelled they came here. India is one of the most tolerant places in the world.'

Sarah's family originated from Germany. 'We are all Orthodox in this community. We observe all the special days, we speak Hebrew as well as English and Malayalam (the language of Kerala) and I keep a perfectly kosher kitchen.' In her limited spare time, Sarah sews sequins on to yarmulkes (skull caps) and sells them to passing tourists.

The community has no rabbi but, as its eldest male member, Jacob is permitted to perform ceremonies at the synagogue. 'Our synagogue is sacred to us but it has become more like a museum than a place of worship,' he says with some remorse. 'I don't know why all the young people had to leave for Israel. Every time another member departs, our hearts break — but what can you do? You cannot stop them.'

In 1972 the Cohens made their first and only visit to Israel. 'We stayed for three months and enjoyed it immensely,' says Sarah. 'I felt really proud to be in the land of my forefathers but we were equally pleased to come home to India,' adds Jacob. 'We are Indians first and then Jews. That is why we stay here.'

Peter Davis

TRIBAL RELIGIONS

Tribal people are found scattered throughout India but with some concentration in the central north. Their origins are hidden but ancient. There has always been some mutual interaction between tribal people and the dominant religions. Many of the most basic tenets of Hinduism possibly originated in tribal culture.

In recent decades, tribal people have been forced to leave their traditional lands due to irrigation works, mining and forestry.

LEFT
A tribal spiritual leader and
shrine in Raya village, Rajasthan

RIGHT
Tribal women, Pushkar, Rajasthan

ZOROASTRIANISM

Zoroastrianism had its inception in Persia and was certainly known to the ancient Greeks. It influenced the evolution of Judaism and Christianity, particularly its concepts of heaven and hell. Zoroaster (Zarathustra) himself was a priest about whom little is known except that he lived in eastern Persia. The religion that bears his name became the state religion of the region now known as Iran and remained so for some 1200 years.

Parsi fire temple, Mumbai. Fire is worshipped as a symbol of God.

Zoroastrianism has a dualistic nature: good and evil are locked in continual battle, with good always triumphing. While Zoroastrianism leans towards monotheism, it isn't quite monotheistic: good and evil entities co-exist, although believers are enjoined to honour only the good. Humanity therefore has a choice; purity is achieved by avoiding contamination by dead matter and things pertaining to death. Unlike Christianity, there is no conflict within the individual between body and soul; both are united in the good versus evil struggle. Zoroastrianism therefore rejects such practices as fasting and celibacy except in purely ritualistic circumstances. Humans, although mortal, have components such as the soul which are timeless. One's prospects for a pleasant afterlife depend on one's deeds, words and thoughts during one's earthly existence. But not every lapse is entered on the balance sheet and the errant soul is not called to account on the day of judgement for each and every mis-demeanour.

Zoroastrianism was eclipsed in Persia by the rise of Islam in the seventh century and its followers, many of whom openly resisted Islam, suffered persecution. In the tenth century some emigrated to India, where they became known as Parsis (Persians). The Parsis settled in Gujarat, becoming farmers and adopting the Gujarati language. When the British ruled India the Parsis moved into commerce and industry, forming a prosperous community in Bombay (the Tata family is one example). The Parsis adopted many British customs including Western dress and banned child marriages.

Sacred fire and sacrifice still play a fundamental role in Zoroastrian ritual. But perhaps the most famous practice involves the 'Towers of Silence'. The Tower of Silence plays an important role in the rituals surrounding death. It is composed of three concentric circles (one each for men, women and children). The corpse is placed within, naked, and exposed to vultures, who pick the bones clean. The bones, once they have been dried by the sun, are swept into a central well. The fourth day of the death rites is the most important for it is on this day that the deceased's soul reaches the next world and presents itself before the deities for judgement.

Parsis may only marry other Parsis, and there are only about 85,000 left in India. But they remain economically and politically influential.

GLOSSARY

H = Hindu   B = Buddhism   C = Christianity
I = Islam   J = Jainism   Z = Zoroastrianism
S = Sikhism   Ju = Judaism

agni fire; a major deity in the Vedas; mediator between humankind and the gods (H)

ahimsa principle of non-violence in thought and deed (H, J, B)

Allah God (I)

amrit/a nectar (S,H)

Ananta serpent-king on whose coils Vishnu rests (H)

Ashoka third-century leader of the Mauryan empire that encompassed almost the entire subcontinent. He converted to Buddhism in 262 BC and inscribed his ethical tenets on rock edicts

ashram 'place of striving'; spiritual community or retreat (H)

Bahubali son of the first tirthankar, or Jain teacher-saint, Adinath. Bahubali engaged in a battle with his brother for his father's kingdom. However, as he was about to strike his brother down, he was overcome with remorse. Renouncing his inheritance, he embarked on a quest for enlightenment, refusing to budge until he had attained moksha (J)

bar mitzvah initiation ceremony for males (Ju)

Bhagavad Gita literally: Song of God; Krishna's lessons to Arjuna, in the form of a dialogue about the nature of duty. Arjuna is reluctant to enter into battle with his kinsfolk, the Kauravas, the battle related in the Mahabharata. Krishna tells Arjuna that as a warrior, it is his dharma to fight, and by doing so, he is offering devotion (bhakti) to God (H)

bhakti ecstatic devotion to a personal god (H)

Bharata Natyam classical dance form of South India, usually performed by women (H)

bindi small dot worn on the forehead by Indian women (H)

Brahma The Creator; one of the Hindu trimurti that also includes Shiva and Vishnu (H)

Brahman the absolute; the Ultimate Principle, Godhead (H)

bodhi tree tree under which the Buddha attained enlightenment (B)

Bollywood India's answer to Hollywood; the film studios of Mumbai (Bombay)

Brahmin person belonging to the priestly caste; one of the four varnas, or castes, in Hindu society (H)

Buddha 'Awakened One'; originator of Buddhism who lived in the fifth century BC; regarded by Hindus as the ninth incarnation of Vishnu (B)

caste system integral hierarchical structure of Hindu society (H)

challot plaited Jewish bread traditionally eaten at Sabbath meals (Ju)

chaam lama dance (H)

chandan sandalwood (H)

chandra moon (H)

Chenmizang one of the Lokapala, the Guardian King of the West (B)

Dalit literally: oppressed; casteless member of Hindu society (H)

darshan literally: glimpse of God; an audience with a guru; viewing of a deity (H)

Dasi Attam original name of the south Indian dance form Bharata Natyam (H)

deva god (H)

devadasi traditionally, female temple dancers (H)

Devi Mother Goddess (H)

dharma duty; appropriate behaviour for one's station in life (H)

Dhev-bumi home of the gods; the Himalaya (H)

Dravidian the original inhabitants of India, pushed south in the second millennium BC by the Indo-Europeans. Adjective used to describe the distinctive temple architecture of South India

Durga form of Shiva's consort Devi, a beautiful but fierce goddess riding a tiger (H)

Durga Puja festival that celebrates the slaying of the buffalo-headed demon Mahishasura by Durga, the benign aspect of the Mother Goddess; widely observed in West Bengal (H)

Eid-ul-Fitr feast celebrating the end of the holy month of fasting, Ramadan (I)

eidy gifts in the form of money usually given to children during the feast of Eid-ul-Fitr (I)

Ganesh elephant-headed god of prosperity and wisdom, the son of Shiva and Parvati (H)

Ganga goddess of the Ganges River (H)

ganga jal water from the holy Ganges River (H)

Garuda Vishnu's half-man, half-bird vehicle (H)

Golden Temple holiest shrine of the Sikhs in India (S)

Gomateshvara Bahubali, son of Adinath, the first Jain tirthankar (teacher-saint) (J)

gompa Tibetan Buddhist monastery (B)

Gopal Krishna as a young boy (H)

gopis milkmaids; Krishna cavorted with them in the forests of Mathura (H)

gopuram soaring pyramidal gateway tower of a Dravidian temple (H)

Granth Sahib holy book – the Sikhs' only object of worship (S)

granthi priest (S)

Gurbani holy scriptures from the Granth Sahib (S)

guru 'dispeller of darkness', 'heavy with wisdom'; teacher or holy person (H, S)

Guru Arjan fifth Sikh guru and first Sikh martyr (S)

gurudwara temple (S)

Guru Gobind Singh tenth guru; founded the Khalsa, the sacred military brotherhood (S)

Guru Nanak first Sikh guru (S)

guru-ka-langar gurudwara kitchen-cum-eating-place, run by volunteers (S)

hajj pilgrimage to Mecca; one of the Five Pillars of Islam (I)

Hanuman popular monkey god; servant of Rama in the Ramayana (H)

imam religious leader (I)

Jama Masjid Friday (main) mosque (I)

Jatakas tales of the past lives of the Buddha (B)

kaccha loose underpants; one of the five kakkars (S)

kakkars five symbols that distinguish Sikh men; they denote the Khalsa, or Sikh brotherhood, and include: karra, kaccha, kangha, kesh and kirpan (S)

Kali 'The Black'; a terrible form of Shiva's wife Devi. She has black skin, drips with blood, is surrounded by snakes and wears a necklace of skulls (H)

kangha comb; one of the five kakkars (S)

karma conduct or action; the law of cause and effect (H)

karman matter generated by one's actions that binds itself to the soul (J)

karra steel bangle; one of the five kakkars (S)

Kartikiya another name for Murugan, Shiva and Parvati's second son, and the god of war (H)

Kartik Purnima auspicious full moon day (October/ November) when thousands of pilgrims converge on Pushkar, in Rajasthan, to bathe in the holy lake (H)

Kashi another name for the sacred city of Varanasi (also called Benares), on the banks of the Ganges (H)

Kathakali classical theatrical dance-drama of Kerala (H)

kesh uncut beard and hair of Sikh men; one of the five kakkars (S)

Khalistan the homeland sought by some Sikhs (S)

Khalsa Sikh brotherhood (S)

kirpan sabre or sword carried by Sikh men; sometimes it appears as an image on the kangha, or comb; it is one of the five kakkars (S)

kirtan hymn-singing (S, H)

Koran sacred text (I)

Krishna Vishnu's eighth incarnation, often coloured blue; a popular Hindu deity (H)

Kshatriya Hindu of the warrior caste; one of the four varnas, or castes, of Hindu society (H)

kumbh pitcher (H)

Kumbh Mela festival held every three years in rotation at Nasik, Ujjain, Allahabad and Haridwar, which attracts literally millions of pilgrims (H)

Lakshmana brother of Rama, whom he assisted in the battle with the demon-king of Lanka, Ravana (H)

Lakshmi Vishnu's consort; the goddess of wealth and prosperity (H)

lingam phallic symbol; symbol of Shiva (H)

Lokapala a Guardian King; they protect the universe and the heavens against outer demons (B)

Mahabharata great Vedic epic of the Bharata Dynasty; an epic poem of about 10,000 verses, describing the battle between the Pandavas and the Kauravas (H)

Mahavira founder of Jainism, a contemporary of the Buddha (J)

Mahayana great-vehicle Buddhism; in this tradition, the Buddha's teachings are adapted to place and time, making the attainment of enlightenment more accessible to lay people (B)

mala garland (H)

mandir temple (H)

mantra sacred word or syllable chanted to aid concentration (H, B)

Makhasankranti festival day on which pilgrims bathe in rivers and tanks, and pay homage to Surya, the sun god. It is considered auspicious to give alms to the poor on this day (H)

masjid mosque (I)

Mecca sacred pilgrimage centre in Saudi Arabia (I)

mela festival, fair (H)

minyan quorum necessary — ten men — for a full prayer service (Ju)

mohalla district of a town or city (I)

Mohammed the Prophet; founder of Islam; he received revelations from Allah (God), which were later compiled in the Koran (I)

moksha spiritual enlightenment; escape from the cycle of birth and death (H, J, B)

morpicchi whiskbroom used by some Jain sects (J)

moulana religious teacher (I)

Murugan second son of Shiva and Parvati, also known as Skanda; widely worshipped in South India (H)

Muslim adherent of the Islamic faith (I)

naga baba naked sadhu (H)

naga stone snake stone; in south India, they depict the spiritually potent cobra (H)

namaskar a greeting; literally: 'I greet the god in you' (H)

Nanda Devi mountain in the Indian Himalaya, and the goddess worshipped by the people of this region (H)

Narayan incarnation of Vishnu with four arms (H)

Nataraja Shiva as Lord of the Cosmic Dance. In this form, he dances away evil and ignorance. The circle of fire surrounding him symbolises the eternal flux of the universe. Creation is energised by the beat of the drum held in Shiva's upper right hand. His other right hand has the palm held out in a gesture of reassurance and protection. His right foot tramples on a dwarf representing ignorance, and his left hand points to his outstretched foot, granting solace and balance (H)

nirvana ultimate aim of existence, final release from the cycle of birth and death (H, B)

Nishan Sahib Sikh flag (S)

om sacred mantra or invocation representing the absolute essence of the divine principle. For Hindus, it is considered to be the aural manifestation of Brahman; for Buddhists, if repeated often enough with complete concentration, it should lead to a state of emptiness (H, B)

Osho also known as Bhagwan Shree Rajneesh; one of India's most popular and flamboyant export gurus (H)

Pandavas heroes of the Mahabharata, the 'Great Battle of Bharata' (ie India), in which they fought with their kinsfolk, the Kauravas (H)

parkarma walkway surrounding a gurudwara (S)

Parsi literally: Persian; adherent of the Zoroastrian faith (Z)

Parvati Daughter of the Mountain; Shiva's wife (H)

Passover festival celebrating the passing over, or sparing, of the Israelites of Egypt when God condemned the first born sons of the Egyptians (Ju)

Pesach Hebrew name for the festival of Passover (Ju)

pinchi whiskbroom used by some sects (J)

pipal sacred tree thought to represent Brahma (H)

pranam respectful salutation (H)

prasaad sweet substance of flour, sugar and ghee, used as a temple offering (H)

puja literally: respect; offering or prayers (H)

Radha head of the gopis; consort of Krishna (H)

Rama seventh incarnation of Vishnu; hero of the Ramayana (H)

Ramadan holy month of fasting during which Muslims abstain from eating, drinking and smoking between sunrise and sunset, and practise sexual abstinence (I)

Ramakrishna nineteenth-century Bengali guru-saint (H)

Ramayana epic which tells the story of Rama and Sita and their conflict with Ravana, the demon-king of Lanka (H)

Ravana demon-king of Lanka; he abducted Sita, wife of Rama, and the titanic battle between him and Rama is told in the Ramayana (H)

rudraksh malas prayer beads comprising 108 rudraksh seeds used by devotees of Shiva (H)

Rukmani one of the consorts of Krishna (H)

sadhu ascetic (H)

Sai Baba widely renowned guru who attracts both Indian and Western followers (H)

salat prayer; one of the Five Pillars of Islam (I)

samadhi place where a holy person has been buried or cremated; also, union with god, enlightenment (H, S)

samsara cyclical nature of existence; the endless cycle of rebirths (H, B)

sangat congregation of worshippers (S)

Sanskrit language in which the Vedas are written; it is the oldest language in the world (H)

Saraswati consort of Brahma. Saraswati is the goddess of learning and music; she usually sits on a white swan and holds a stringed instrument called a veena (H)

sarowar sacred pool; tank (S)

Sati wife of Shiva, who immolated herself after he was insulted by her father. The practice of sati (self-immolation by a widow on her husband's funeral pyre) has been banned for more than a century (H)

saum fasting; one of the Five Pillars of Islam (I)

sewa voluntary service (S)

sewadaar volunteer (S)

shabad hymn (S)

shahadah declaration of faith: There is no god but Allah; Mohammed is his prophet'; one of the Five Pillars of Islam (I)

Shah Jahan Mughal emperor who lived in the seventeenth century; responsible for building Delhi's massive Jama Masjid, and the Taj Mahal in Agra, a mausoleum for his wife Mumtaz, who died in childbirth (I)

Shaikh Hazrat Nizam-ud-din Aulia Chisti Sufi saint of the Chistia order (I)

Shaivite devotee of Shiva (H)

Shakti consort of Shiva; also divine energy (H)

She'ma prayer (Ju)

Shiva one of the Hindu trimurti that includes Brahma and Vishnu; god of destruction and creation (H)

Siddhartha Gautama birth name of the Buddha (B)

sindoor vermilion (H)

Singh name bestowed by Guru Gobind Singh on Sikhs belonging to the Khalsa, or sacred military brotherhood; common name of all male Sikhs (S)

Sita consort of Rama; in the Ramayana, she was abducted by the demon-king of Lanka, Ravana (H)

St Thomas the Apostle according to tradition, 'Doubting Thomas' brought Christianity to India in 52 AD (C)

stupas hemispherical monuments, many containing relics of the Buddha or Buddhist saints (B)

Sudra member of the peasant caste; one of the four varnas, or castes, of Hindu society (H)

Sufi adherent of the Muslim mystical order (I)

Surya sun god (H)

Thaipusam festival celebrated in South India at which Murugan, second son of Shiva and Parvati, is worshipped. Some devotees undergo severe austerities in order to atone for accumulated bad karma (H)

thakur ghar literally: home for the gods; place within a home set aside for puja (worship) (H)

Theravada literally 'word of the elders'; Buddhist school of thought that contends that the teachings of the Buddha should be preserved and practised in their original forms (B)

tika forehead mark worn by women (H)

tilak forehead mark worn by devout Hindu men (H)

tirtha literally: crossing place; a sacred place where humans can apprehend the divine, and the gods can cross over to earth; often it is at the site of a river confluence (H)

torana elaborately sculpted freestanding gateway (B)

Tower of Silence place where the dead are laid to be consumed by vultures, in order not to contaminate the sacred elements of earth, fire, air and water (Z)

trimurti Hindu trinity of Brahma, Shiva and Vishnu; the three representations of Brahman (H)

trishul trident; Shiva carries one (H)

tulsi basil (H)

Untouchables former name of the Dalits, the casteless members of Hindu society (H)

Vaishnavite devotee of Vishnu (H)

Vaisya Hindu of the merchant caste; one of the four varnas, or castes, of Hindu society (H)

Varanasi one of the holiest cities in India; also known as Kashi, or Benares. To die here is to attain instant moksha, or release from the cycle of birth and death (H)

varna caste (H)

Vasant Panchami spring festival at which Saraswati, the goddess of learning and music, is worshipped (H)

Vedas Hindu sacred books; a collection of hymns composed in pre-classical Sanskrit during the second millennium BC and divided into four books: Rig-Veda (the oldest), Yajur-Veda, Sama-Veda and Atharva-Veda (H)

vibhuti ash; worn on the forehead by some devout Hindus (H)

vimana tower over the central shrine of a mandir; in South India, it is stepped as opposed to curvilinear (H)

Vishnu one of the trimurti that also includes Shiva and Brahma; Vishnu is the preserver or sustainer; he has to date had nine incarnations, including Rama (of the Ramayana), Krishna and the Buddha (H)

Vivekananda widely revered Bengali guru-saint (H)

yarmulke skull cap (Ju)

wuzoo ritual washing undertaken before prayer (I)

yatra pilgrimage (H)

zakat alms giving; one of the Five Pillars of Islam (I)

Zarathustra alternative form of Zoroaster (Z)

Zoroaster Persian priest, founder of Zoroastrianism (Z)

THE PEOPLE BEHIND SACRED INDIA

William Dalrymple

Award-winning English travel writer William Dalrymple is intimately acquainted with the subcontinent. He spent five years in India researching *City of Djinns*, which won the 1994 Thomas Cook Travel Book Award and the *Sunday Times* Young British Writer of the Year Award. He received further accolades for his next book, *From the Holy Mountain*. William potently evokes the mystery and colour of India's religious life in his foreword.

Major Contributors

Most of the major contributors come from within Lonely Planet's own ranks; Hindu, Sikh and Muslim, they are as diverse as their subject.

Sharan Kaur was born in Malaysia and has had a long career in publishing both in Malaysia and Australia. Raised in the Sikh culture, she has a passionate interest in all classical Indian music. Working on Sacred India offered her the opportunity to realise her long-held wish to visit the Golden Temple and also to refresh her family ties. Sharan is the senior editor responsible for Lonely Planet's guidebooks to the Indian subcontinent.

Masood Hayat was born in Delhi but fled India with his parents at the time of Partition. He grew up in Karachi and, after completing his secondary education, left for the UK where he studied accountancy. He combined work in London with extensive travel in Europe, the Middle East and Asia before moving to Australia where he married and operated hotels and restaurants. Mas relaxes by walking his stout beagle, Ben, along the banks of Melbourne's Yarra River and enjoys piloting small planes whenever he can.

After completing a business degree in Melbourne, a deep passion for travel lured Sarina Singh to India. There she trained as a hotel manager but later drifted into journalism, working as a freelance journalist and foreign correspondent. After three and a half years in India, Sarina returned to Australia, undertook a postgraduate journalism course and wrote two television documentary scripts. Lonely Planet guidebooks to which she has contributed include *India, Rajasthan, Africa* and *Mauritius, Réunion & Seychelles*.

Meera Govil was born in Dehra Dun, a town nestled in the Himalayan foothills. She grew up in Delhi happily surrounded by a very extended family. After marrying her childhood sweetheart, Meera wrote for children's magazines, taught English, led academic travellers around India and now works in her own dream bookshop in Melbourne. Committed to her local community, her other loves are her family and long walks without heavy backpacks.

Born in the UK and raised in Australia, Susan Mitra was eighteen when she first visited India. Since then she has visited India regularly, spending time with her family and friends and travelling extensively through the country she loves. Susan studied Indian politics and history at university and has a keen interest in Indian culture, particularly music, dance and food. During her career with Lonely Planet she has worked as managing editor, US publishing manager and is presently manager of human resources.

Richard I'Anson's photography is widely exhibited and published, and has featured in more than one hundred editions of Lonely Planet titles, including *Chasing Rickshaws*, Lonely Planet's first pictorial book. He first travelled to India in 1986 and has been continually drawn back, attracted by the country's colour and intensity. Richard is tempted to believe that he may return as a sadhu in a future life. He realises in his more pragmatic moments that the closest he will come to a dedicated spiritual life is photographing those who pursue one.

Other contributors include Teresa Cannon, Michelle Coxall, Peter Davis, Paul Harding, Eytan Uliel, Don Miller and Carolyn Papworth. Kelli Hamblet created the line illustrations.

Other photographers include Paul Beinssen, Peter Davis, Greg Elms, Paul Harding, Chris Mellor, Sarina Singh and Liz Thompson.

This book would not have been possible without the insights and stories from the many Indian people we met — in homes, places of worship and on the road. Particular thanks from Sarina Singh to Manohar Singh and Arvind Singh Mewar for taking so much time to share their stories. Susan Mitra thanks Thakuma, Dipen, Gill, Kutti Kaka, Kajal Kakima, Jethu and Boroma. Special thanks from Sharan Kaur to the staff at the Information Office, Golden Temple, Amritsar; to Rajinder, Tej, Raam, Tinu, Manu and their families in India; and to Sue Galley, who bullied her into this project. Richard I'Anson extends his gratitude to Sharan and Susan for carrying all his bags and equipment. Susan and Sharan thank Richard for travelling light.

Lonely Planet has been exploring India for over twenty five years. To produce this book we drew on the experiences of LP authors and editors such as Hugh Finlay, Jane Rawson and Christine Niven. We also sent a small team of writers, an illustrator and a photographer to capture the present mood and complexity of India's religions.

This book was produced in Lonely Planet's Melbourne office. It was designed by Jamieson Gross who met every awful deadline we threw at him. Thanks Jamo. Kate Ferris relentlessly scanned the photographs and was also a stickler for deadlines. Tamsin Wilson, Lonely Planet's design manager, calmly provided ongoing support and sound advice, as did Valerie Tellini. The project was conceived by Sue Galley, managed by Susan Keogh and edited by Michelle Coxall. Printing was supervised by Graham Imeson. The map was drawn by Jim Miller. Thanks also to the following people for support: Richard Everist, John Dennithorne, Carolyn Papworth, Tim Uden, Elissa Coffman and Simon Bracken.

Sharan Kaur and Susan Mitra interviewing staff and pilgrims at the Golden Temple, Amritsar

PHOTO CREDITS

Richard I'Anson p3, p7 top left, p7 bottom right, p9, p12, p13 left, p13 top right, p13 bottom right, p22 left, p22 centre, p22 right, p23, p24 bottom, p27, p28 top, p28 bottom, p29, p30, p35, p37, p42, p43, p46 top, p46 bottom, p49, p50, p51, p52 left, p52 right, p53, p56 left, p58, p60, p61 top, p61 bottom, p63, p64, p65, p70, p71, p72, p75, p76, p77, p79, p82, p83, p84, p85, p86, p87 left, p87 top right, p87 bottom right, p89, p90, p91, p92, p93, p94 left, p94 right, p95, p96, p99, p100, p101 top, p101 bottom, p102, p103, p107, p108, p109, p110, p111 left, p111 top right, p111 bottom right, p112, p113 top left, p113 bottom left, p113 top right, p113 bottom right, p114, p115, p117, p118, p121, p122 top, p123 left, p123 right, p128, p130, p131 top right, p131 bottom right, p132, p133, p135, p138 left, p138 right, p143, p144, p146, p149, p150 bottom, p153

Biddy Baxter p17 right

Bryn Thomas p17 left

Chris Mellor p24 top, p78

David Collins p134 far left, p134 left, p152 bottom, p158

Eddie Gerald p4 bottom, p10, p11, p16 left, p21, p25, p26, p39, p47, p66, p67 top, p67 bottom, p68 right, p69, p 88, p140

Greg Elms p14 right, p15, p40, p154

Karen Trist p145 bottom right, p159

Lindsay Brown p142

Liz Thompson p6, p48, p68 left, p134, p135, p150 top, p151, p156 top left, p156 bottom right

Mark Daffy p137

Paul Beinssen p1, p8, p14 left, p38, p44 left, p45, p54 top, p55, p56 right, p57

Paul Harding p124 top centre, p124 bottom left, p124 bottom right, p125, p139 left, p139 top right, p139 bottom right, p141, p147, p148

Peter Davis p4 top, p16 right, p62, p145 top left, p152 top, p155 top, p155 bottom

Sarah-Jane Cleland p5, p20, p32, p33, p34, p122 bottom, p157

Sanjay Singh p54 bottom

Sarina Singh p59

Steve Davey p44 right

The photographs in this book are available from
Lonely Planet Images
email: lpi@lonelyplanet.com.au